The Beginning of the
World of Books
1450 to 1470

The Beginning of the
World of Books
1450 to 1470

*A Chronological Survey of the Texts chosen
for Printing during the First Twenty Years
of the Printing Art*

*With a Synopsis of the
Gutenberg Documents*

Margaret Bingham Stillwell

*The Bibliographical Society
of America
New York · 1972*

Publication of the Lathrop Colgate Harper Litt.D. Trust Fund

To

FREDERICK RICHMOND GOFF

Chief of the Rare Book Division
The Library of Congress
who began his Career
as my Student and Assistant and now
more than Thirty Years later
has generously aided in
gathering this Data

Contents

Pages

PRELIMINARY SECTIONS
   Preface — ix
   Methodology — xv
   Acknowledgments — xix
   Abbreviations, Symbols, and Terms — xxi

BOOKS AND BROADSIDES, 1450 to 1470 — I
   A Chronological Survey of the Texts chosen for Printing during the First Twenty Years of the Printing Art

SUPPLEMENTARY SECTIONS
   Authors by Periods — 59
   Commentators, Editors, and Translators — 61
   Subject Analysis of Early Books and Broadsides — 63
   Typographical Analyses of Imprints before 1470:
      Early Imprints of Controversial Origin — 65
      Printers and Presses before 1470 — 65
      Printing Towns before 1470 — 66
   Undated Imprints currently unassigned, or re-assigned to 1470 or later — 68

APPENDIXES
   The Gutenberg Documents: *Notes on Documentary Sources relative to Johann Gensfleisch zur Laden zu Gutenberg, c. 1399–1467/68*
      Subject Analysis — 74
      Notes on the Manuscript Records, 1420–1468 — 75
      Printed Statements, 1468–1499 — 89
   Undated Imprints assigned to The Netherlands — 97

INDEX — 107

Preface

For a hundred years or more the bibliographical scholars of the world have sought to identify the man of genius who, in the mid-fifteenth century, changed the course of civilization by introducing the art of printing into the Western World.

Not only has Johann Gutenberg of Mainz been proclaimed as the inventor, but in the zeal of local or family pride the names of Lourens Janszoon Coster of Haarlem, Nicolaus Jenson of Venice, Pamfilo Castaldi of Feltre, Johann Mentelin of Strasbourg, Prokop Waldfoghel of Avignon, Jean Brito of Bruges, and Johann Fust of Mainz have each been presented as a candidate for that honor. In the course of the years, these claims have been studied and sifted with infinite care, often in heated contention. Gradually, however, the hot glow of controversy has cooled. Rival claims have been disposed of one by one, and it is to Gutenberg that we pay tribute today.

Our knowledge of him and of his claim rests upon two factors. First, upon a series of documents in manuscript that range from 1420 to the settling of his estate in 1468. These, however, fail to give conclusive support to his claim as the inventor of printing, although presenting in the early records an occasional, vague reference to printing, paper, ink, a press, and "four pieces" which Mr. Theodore Low DeVinne, Dr. Otto W. Fuhrmann and others have identified as the parts of a type-casting mould.

The second factor consists of tributes to Gutenberg by his contemporaries and their successors, which specifically name him as the inventor of printing in statements which appeared in printed books issued during the years 1470–1499. Added support for Gutenberg comes from his partner's grandson, Johann Schoeffer, who in the preface to his 1523 edition of Livy stated that printing was invented by Johann Gutenberg at Mainz in 1450 and later improved upon by Johann Fust and Peter Schoeffer. Taken together, the documents and these printed statements would seem to make Gutenberg's position unassailable.

Although the claim of Coster of Haarlem is generally disallowed, after a prolonged controversy between German scholars and those of Holland, it is true that there exists a group of unsigned, undated, and unidentified pieces assigned to The Netherlands. These items stand apart from all others, a complete enigma. Many of them are fragments found in the bindings of fifteenth-century books located in Holland. In heavy types otherwise unknown, they give no clue to their origin, in spite of the immense amount of study that has been lavished upon them.

In intriguing contrast to the primitive appearance of these early pieces is the sophisticated choice of some of the titles. These are not catch-penny booklets printed for sale at a Lenten Fair. Apart from various printings of Donatus, an ABC for the use of children, various editions of the *Doctrinale* and the *Speculum humanae salvationis*, and a few religious manuals, these others, so it would seem, were for the use of men of the world—produced perhaps by a humanist or two who enjoyed experimenting with the new mechanical device, as did Joannes Philippi de Lignamine, the papal physician who had a press for his own use set up in Rome about 1470, that he might print books for himself and his friends. At any rate, here we have Petrarch's *De salibus virorum illustrium*; Aesop's *Fabulae* translated from the Greek by Lorenzo Valla; the *Singularia in causis criminalibus* by Ludovicus Pontanus, a jurist of Rome, Siena, and Florence; Homer's *Iliad* in Latin verse, translated from the abridgment then attributed to Pindar; and the medical work *De salute corporis* by Guglielmo de Saliceto.

Whatever their origin and period, these early pieces assigned to The Netherlands—and the more sophisticated titles very likely printed in one or more of the cultural centers—are typographically unrelated to other early pieces. They are unrelated, also, to other printing in The Netherlands, where a press is definitely known to have been established in 1473. Chronologically some of these titles have been assigned to 1470 or later. Hence they do not come within the scope of the present volume. None of these assignments, however, is conclusive. It is even possible that some of the unassigned pieces may date from before 1470. This is true, for instance, of the first Latin edition of the *Speculum humanae salvationis* which Mr. Allan Stevenson, from a study of the paper, assigns to [*c.* 1468]. It is because of these uncertainties that the titles in this group—formerly known as Costeriana—are here listed tentatively and apart, in Appendix B.

The year 1470 was a turning-point in the history of printing. Twenty years had passed since the invention of movable metal type. The printing art had been introduced and gradually accepted. There had come an awakening to the intellectual value and the commercial possibilities of the mechanical reproduction of texts. In 1470 there began the so-called triumphant march of printing. Up to that year—except for brief introduction in Subiaco, Rome,

Basel, and Venice—printing had centered in Germany. During 1470, however, and from that time onward, the printing art spread rapidly throughout
Europe. But that is an entirely different story from that of the period covered
here.

It is with the period before 1470, that this monograph deals. For the
moment at least, controversy regarding early date-assignments seems to have
reached a stopping-place. New knowledge is sure to be brought to light from
time to time. But, as opposed to the long years of futile hypotheses, it would
seem that a plateau of understanding has now been reached, which rests upon
a sound bibliographic base. It is this modern point of view and the reasons for
it that I have endeavored to summarize here and to present in simple terms,
shorn of the suppositions of the past.

The "controversialists" of our time, although one should no longer call
them that, seek to base their conclusions upon documentary evidence or upon
typographical evidence revealed by the books themselves, rather than upon
the hypotheses which formerly blurred and confused the issues.

In spite of the stupendous job accomplished by bibliographers in the first
half of our century in identifying, organizing, and describing incunabula
meticulously and accurately, the treatises written regarding the introductory
period of printing remained largely hypothetical. In discussing the few documentary sources that exist, the incunabulists of that period tended to take off
on flights of their own conjecture, thus creating sad confusion. Added to this
was the fact that, with the exception of three books, all of those issued during
the first decade of printing were produced anonymously; and not even the
three exceptions contained all of the prerequisites stating place, printer, and
date. Thus there was ample room for conjecture.

Endless treatises were written, no doubt with good intent. But honest
hypotheses tend to degenerate into acceptance as possibility, probability, and
finally as "facts." Myths regarding Gutenberg's career and his associates
hardened into tradition, some of which is repeated to this day, casually and
without question. There have been, however, certain exceptions—bibliographers and bibliophiles determined to keep to the known facts.

General Rush Hawkins, having lived through the years when the question
of who invented printing was a matter of international controversy, had proclaimed himself a "Gutenberg man." He had no use for conjecture. In an
effort to counteract that trend, he had made it a point to include in his collection of incunabula the fifteenth-century books in which Gutenberg was
named to that honor by his contemporaries and their immediate successors.
Apropos of the coming celebration of the five-hundredth anniversary of the
invention of printing, and using this specialized group as a base, I took the

opportunity in 1936 to present these tributes to the inventor, in the original Latin and in English, in my monograph on *Gutenberg and the Catholicon*. Three years later, Dr. Aloys Ruppel presented the contemporary, manuscript records relative to Gutenberg's life and career, in his book on *Johannes Gutenberg, sein Leben und sein Werk*. In 1940, Dr. Otto W. Fuhrmann produced a volume on *Gutenberg and the Strasbourg documents of 1439*, which, in addition to a careful analysis of documents relating to Gutenberg during his experimental years at Strasbourg, included the texts of the documents in the original Alsatian, and in French, German, and English. The following year, Mr. Douglas C. McMurtrie, in his monograph on *The Gutenberg documents with translations of the texts based with authority on the compilation of Dr. Karl Schorbach*, included—for their proper understanding and interpretation—a discussion of legal procedure and usage in the fifteenth century. In a further effort to keep modern concepts down to earth, a summary of the manuscript documents, 1420–1468, and a review of the printed statements, 1468–1499, have been included in the Appendix to the present volume.

As for the identification of the first printed books—in addition to such careful bibliographic assignments as appear in the *Catalogue of books printed in the XVth century now in the British Museum* (started in the early years of our century and still in process of publication), and in the partially published *Gesamtkatalog der Wiegendrucke*—attention has been given by various bibliographers to special groups and imprints. In 1948, for instance, Dr. Carl Wehmer by scientific analysis assigned a group of early pieces to the 1450s, which had hitherto been accepted as of earlier date; and recently through typographical analysis and collation, Mr. George D. Painter has shown these to be of the Gutenbergian system. Through similar analysis, Dr. Kurt Ohly in 1940 submitted that the three earliest Basel imprints [*c.*1468/69] are prior to the local printers' strike of 1471, and accepted the chronological sequence previously assigned by Dr. Victor Scholderer in the British Museum *Catalogue*. Again, in the 1960s, after the discussion of an unsigned *Missale speciale* had elicited close to eighty treatises, a new note—or a scientific approach to an old one—was introduced in an effort to pinpoint the *Missale*'s date through the manufacture and use of the paper on which it was printed. In a meticulous study of this factor, Mr. Allan Stevenson in 1967 produced a massive volume indicating that the *Missale* was printed before 1474. And I have recently learned that Dr. Curt F. Bühler has a paper in process on the relevance of watermarks in determining the date of printing, and another article scheduled to appear in a forthcoming issue of the *Papers* of the Bibliographical Society of America on *The Missale speciale and the Feast of the Presentation of the Blessed Virgin Mary*, the Office for which (promulgated in 1468) is not in the text. In the typescript which he graciously lent me, I find the wholesome statement that his paper, and others that will possibly follow it, "will deal solely with facts—not with opinions, inferences, or hypotheses based on deductions."

Thus, step by step, our knowledge of the first printed books progresses. And around the present plateau of understanding there hovers the cool air of sanity that augurs well for the investigations of the future.

Margaret Bingham Stillwell

Librarian Emerita of the Annmary Brown Memorial
Professor Emerita of Bibliography, Brown University

Elfendale,
Greenville, Rhode Island
22 October, 1971

Methodology

In the main section of the book the entries, in general, follow the pattern introduced in the 1940 census of *Incunabula in American libraries* and established in that of 1964. Brief statements of author, title, place, printer, and date are followed by a block of notes giving bibliographical references [*Ref*:]; the location of rare and unique copies [*Cop*:]; various annotations [*N.B.*:]; the titles of monographs or of articles relating to the work or some aspect of it [*Mon*:]; and the titles of facsimiles reproducing the work as a whole or in part [*Fac*:].

But here, this being a chronology, the entries are listed under successive years, although alphabetically by authors within each year. Variant author-forms are cited in the entries. Author dates are quoted. A list of Abbreviations, Symbols, and Terms precedes the main text. In the belief that each text in a compilation is bibliographically equal in importance to the one that appears first in the volume, the texts are entered separately although each is accompanied by reference to the compilation, in parentheses.

Following the 215 entries which make up the main section of the present volume is a Supplementary Section including a series of analytical lists recording authors by periods; commentators, editors, and translators; a subject analysis; early imprints of controversial origin; printers and presses before 1470; printing towns in which one or more presses were in operation prior to that year; and a list of works hitherto assigned to the introductory period of early printing, but which through bibliographic processes have now been re-assigned to 1470 or later.

In addition there are two Appendices. The first includes a subject-analysis and a chronology summarizing the manuscript records, the so-called Gutenberg documents, from 1420 to the settling of his estate in 1468; together with the printed tributes honoring Gutenberg as the inventor of printing and issued during the years 1470 through 1499. The second appendix presents a list of early, undated pieces assigned to The Netherlands—the Dutch prototypographs formerly known as the "Costeriana." An Index follows, listing authors, anonymous titles, and variant author-forms.

In attempting to list the books and broadsides issued during the first twenty years of the printing art, two areas present special difficulty. The first consists of a small group of unsigned pieces, frequently unique or known only through fragments. These had been accepted traditionally as experimental pieces printed in the 1440s, before the printing of the "Gutenberg Bible" had been undertaken. The only item in this group to which a date had seemed assignable was the so-called "Calendar for 1448" presumably printed toward the end of the preceding year.

A study of the "Calendar" made in 1948 by Dr. Viktor Stegemann, a specialist in medieval astrology, has revealed, however, that it is in reality an astrological table for use in casting horoscopes which, although based upon the position of the planets in 1448, was planned for use during several decades. Thus it may have been printed at any time within that period, rather than shortly before 1448 as had been supposed.

Simultaneous with this analysis and published together with it, a meticulous typographical study of this planet-table, and of the other items in this group, presented by Dr. Carl Wehmer in his monograph on the *Mainzer Probedrucke in der Type des sogenannten astronomischen Kalenders für 1448* (Munchen, 1948), showed reason for re-assigning the group to the 1450s, as a group related to the eponymous press of the *Türkenkalender für 1455* but not, in his opinion, related to Gutenberg. As the result of an equally meticulous typographical analysis of the items within this group, Mr. George D. Painter in a paper on *Gutenberg and the B36 Group: A Re-consideration* has been able to align the items within the group chronologically and to show proof that the group is a part of the Gutenbergian system of type-casting. Salient points presented by both bibliographers are noted below, among the early entries listed under the 1450s.

A second area of difficulty lay in the chronological assignment of the controversial *Missale speciale*. Since the turn of the present century, close to eighty monographs and papers have been published in the effort to assign the *Missale speciale* to place and date. The most recent of these is a treatise of four hundred pages in which Mr. Allan Stevenson, in his monograph on *The Problem of the Missale speciale*, London, 1967, discusses the accumulated hypotheses in detail and presents the results of his own meticulous research. In this and in his essay on *Paper evidence and the Missale speciale* (*Gutenberg-Jahrbuch*, 1962), Mr. Stevenson shows reason for assigning the *Missale speciale* to about 1473 or the early part of 1474, and its abridgment—the *Missale abbreviatum*—to possibly a slightly earlier date. Since his study of the period of the paper on which these items were printed presents more tangible evidence than the earlier, hypothetical assignments to the year 1454, the late 1450s, or the 1460s, entries for these works have been placed in a supplementary section listing *Undated Imprints currently unassigned, or re-assigned to 1470 or later.* [The question, however, is still an open one, for Dr. Curt F. Bühler, as noted above in the Preface, has a paper which is scheduled to appear in a forthcoming issue of the *Papers* of the Bibliographical Society of America, and a possible series of articles on the *Missale speciale* to appear in the future.]

Another area of difficulty was simplified by the publication in 1966 of *The Fifteenth-century printing types of the Low Countries* by Wytse and Lotte Hellinga. References to their type-classifications, resulting from the typographical analysis of the early primitive pieces of printing found in Holland (the former so-called Costeriana), are cited here under the entries for those titles, in Appendix B: *Undated imprints assigned to the Netherlands.*

Acknowledgments

In the Preface of my first book on incunabula, published some forty years ago, I find that I wrote, "Among other workers in the field, the owners of rare books, and the scholars devoted to the theme, one finds coöperation and a friendly spirit." During the intervening years this has proved more than true. In the present instance, my warmest thanks are due Dr. Victor Scholderer of the British Museum and Dr. Curt F. Bühler of the Pierpont Morgan Library, for various suggestions given me in the early stages of this work. And now, as I complete my task, I find myself deeply indebted to Mr. George D. Painter, Assistant Keeper of Printed Books at the British Museum, for his scrutiny of my text, helpful data, and the galley-proofs of his forthcoming paper on *Gutenberg and the B36 Group: A Re-consideration*, which have enabled me to include mention of the results of the most recent research in this controversial field. It is a pleasure to note, also, the keen interest in the typographical aspects of this volume shown by Mr. Gabriel Austin, chairman of the Publications Committee of the Bibliographical Society of America.

I find that, when you have retired from a university with its endless resources and seek the benefits of country life for a quiet continuance of your writing, the conditions under which you work eventually change. Distance, which at first seemed of little moment, becomes a handicap. And miles of traffic suddenly debar you from the books you need for daily use. I am therefore greatly indebted to Dr. Stuart C. Sherman, Librarian of the John Hay Library, Brown University, who has graciously supplied data on such points as awaited last minute verification, or has brought to my home reference material needed for the final checking of the text. And here I have had the unremitting aid of my housemate, Dorothy Carter Allan, in preparing the typescript for the press. There is a deep sense of companionship which comes from working together on a closely knit project, an enrichment of association which is attainable in no other way.

Ackowledgments

To these good friends I give sincerest thanks—as also to Dr. Frederick R. Goff, Chief of the Rare Book Division of the Library of Congress, whose courtesy is noted in the Dedication, although not so fully nor so graciously as is deserved. His keen and helpful interest—as in the days when we worked together on the 1940 census of *Incunabula in American Libraries*—has given me the privilege of enjoying once again the rapport of that earlier time.

M. B. S.

Abbreviations, Symbols, and Terms

Abbreviations

AmBCat	Annmary Brown Memorial. Catalogue of books . . . from the presses of the first printers, collected by Rush C. Hawkins . . . Catalogued by Alfred W. Pollard. Oxford, 1910.
BMC	British Museum. Catalogue of books printed in the fifteenth century now in the British Museum. Parts I–IX, London, 1908–1962. (Lithographed reprint with annotations, parts I–VIII, London, 1963; part IX, 1967.)
Bradshaw	Bradshaw, Henry. A Classified index of the fifteenth century books in the collection of the late M. J. DeMeyer. Memoranda II. London, 1870. (Reprinted in Bradshaw's *Collected papers*, Cambridge, 1889.)
BSA	Bibliographical Society of America, New York.
Bühler	Bühler, Curt F. New Coster fragments of the Doctrinale (Gutenberg Jahrbuch, 1938).
Bühler(ANZ)	Bühler, Curt F. A Note on Zedler's Coster theory (BSA. *Papers*, 37, 1943).
Bühler(FCB)	Bühler, Curt F. Fifteenth century books and the twentieth century. An Address . . . and a catalogue of an exhibition . . . held at The Grolier Club. New York, 1952.
Bühler(MSPr)	Bühler, Curt F. The Missale speciale and the Feast of the Presentation of the Blessed Virgin Mary. (*Seen in advance copy; scheduled to appear in the Papers of the Bibliographical Society of America.*)
Burger	Burger, Konrad. The printers and publishers of the fifteenth century with lists of their works. London, 1902 (in Copinger, part II, London, 1902).
Burger(Buch)	Burger, Konrad. Buchhändlerzeigen des 15. Jahrhunderts, Leipzig, 1907.
Camp	Campbell, W. F. A. G. Annales de la typographie néerlandaise au XVe siècle. La Haye, 1874. Supplements 1–4, 1878–1890. [For revision, see below under: Kron.]

Cen   A term referring to the notations of the Second Census of *Incunabula in American Libraries* which appear in a secondary position in the Third Census and are therefore applicable to both editions. [For the Third Census, see below under: Goff.]

C(Vir)   Copinger, W. A. Incunabula Virgiliana (p. 123–226 in: Bibliographical Society. *Transactions II*. London, 1893–94).

Cop   Copinger, W. A. Supplement of Hain's *Repertorium bibliographicum*. In two parts. London, 1895, 1898, 1902. 2 v. in 3. (Reprinted at Berlin, 1926.)

DeR(M)   Ricci, Seymour de. Catalogue raisonné des premières impressions de Mayence, 1455–67. Mainz, 1911. (Gutenberg-Gesellschaft. *Veröffentlichungen*, VIII–IX.)

Einbl   Einblattdrucke des XV. Jahrhunderts. Ed: Konrad Haebler ... hrsg. von der Kommission für den Gesamtkatalog der Wiegendrucke. Halle, 1914. (Sammlung bibliothekswissenschaftlicher Arbeiten. H. 35–36.)

Fuhrmann   Fuhrmann, Otto W. Gutenberg and the Strasbourg documents of 1439. An interpretation. New York, 1940.

Geldn (Bam)   Geldner, Ferdinand. Die Buchdruckerkunst im alten Bamberg, Bamberg, 1964.

Geldner   Geldner, Ferdinand. Die deutschen Inkunabeldrucke ... Erst Band: Das deutsche Sprachgebiet. Stuttgart, 1968.

Gerardy   Gerardy, Theo. Die Wasserzeichen des mit Gutenbergs kleiner Psaltertype gedruckten Missale speciale (p. 13–22 in: Papiergeschichte 10 1960).

Gerardy(ZD)   Gerardy, Theo. Zur Datierung des mit Gutenbergs kleiner Psaltertype gedruckten Missale speciale (p. 399–415 in: Archiv für Geschichte des Buchwesens 5 1964).

Goff   Goff, Frederick R. Incunabula in American libraries: A third census of fifteenth-century books recorded in North American collections. New York, 1964. (The Bibliographical Society of America.) *With numbers from the Second Census, 1940, cited in secondary position.*

GW   Gesamtkatalog der Wiegendrucke. Vols. 1–8, pt. 1 (A–Fed). Leipzig, 1925–40.

H   Hain, Ludwig. Repertorium bibliographicum, in quo libri omnes ab arte typographica inventa ad annum MD. typi expressi. Stuttgart, 1826–1838. 2 vols. in 4.

HC   Copinger, W. A. Supplement to Hain's *Repertorium bibliographicum*. Part I. London, 1895.

HCR   Reichling, Dietrich. Appendices ad Hainii-Copingeri *Repertorium bibliographicum* ... Emendationes. 6 vols. and index. Monachii, 1905–11. See also below, under: HR.

Abbreviations, Symbols, and Terms

HEHCat — Henry E. Huntington Library. Incunabula in the Huntington Library. [Compiled by Herman R. Mead.] San Marino, 1937.

Hellinga — Hellinga, Wytse and Lotte. The fifteenth-century printing types of the Low Countries. Amsterdam, 1966. 2 vols.

Highet(CT) — Highet, Gilbert. The classical tradition. New York, 1949.

HPT — *An abbreviation frequently used for* Hellinga, *q.v.*

HR — Reichling, Dietrich. Appendices ... Monasterii, 1914. [*For the main work which this supplements, see above, under*: HCR.]

Klebs — Klebs, Arnold C. Incunabula scientifica et medica. Short title list. Bruges, 1938. [Reprinted from *Osiris*, vol. IV.]

Kron — Kronenberg, M. E. Campbell's Annales de la typographie néerlandaise au XVe siècle. Contributions to a new edition. The Hague, 1956.

Kron(More) — Kronenberg, M. E. More contributions ... The Hague, 1964.

LC(LJR.Cat) — Rosenwald, Lessing J. The Rosenwald Collection. A Catalogue of illustrated books and manuscripts, of books from celebrated presses, and of bindings and maps, 1150–1950. The gift of Lessing J. Rosenwald to the Library of Congress. (Ed: Frederick R. Goff.) Washington, 1954.

L-H — Lehmann-Haupt, Hellmut. Peter Schoeffer of Gernsheim and Mainz with a list of his surviving books and broadsides. Rochester, N.Y., 1950.

Nachträge — Nachträge zu Hain's *Repertorium bibliographicum* und seinen Fortsetzungen. Als Probe des Gesamtkatalog der Wiegendrucke, hrsg. von der Kommission für den Gesamtkatalog der Wiegendrucke. Leipzig, 1910.

Oates — A Catalogue of the fifteenth-century printed books in the University Library, Cambridge, compiled by J. C. Oates. Cambridge, 1954.

Osler(IM) — Osler, *Sir* William. Incunabula medica. A study of the earliest printed medical books, 1467-80. Oxford, 1923.

Ottley — Ottley, William Y. An Inquiry concerning the invention of printing. London, 1863.

Painter — Painter, George D. Gutenberg and the B36 Group: A Re-consideration. (*Seen in galley-proof during the preparation of the present volume; and since published as p. 292–322 in*: Essays in honour of Victor Scholderer (Ed: Dennis E. Rhodes).) Mainz, 1970.

Pell — Pellechet, Marie. Catalogue général des incunables des bibliothèques publiques de France. 3 vols. (A–Gregorious Magnus). Paris, 1897–1909. [Posthumous section edited by M. -Louis Polain.]

Piccard — Piccard, G. Die Datierung des Misalle Speciale Constantiense durch seine Papiermarken (*p. 571–584 in*: Archiv für Geschichte des Buch-Wesens, II, 1900).

Polain	Polain, M. -Louis. Catalogue des livres imprimés au quinzieme siècle des bibliothèques de Belgique. 4 vols. Bruxelles, 1932.
Pr	Proctor, Robert. An Index to the early printed books in the British Museum from the invention of printing to the year MD. with notes of those in the Bodleian Library. 2 vols. London, 1898. 4 supplements, 1899–1902.
Ruppel	Ruppel, Aloys. Johannes Gutenberg, sein Leben und sein Werk. Berlin, 1939; Berlin, 1947. Reprinted with a supplementary bibliography, Nieuwkoop, 1967.
Sander	Sander, Max. Le livres à figures italien depuis 1467 jusqu'à 1530, essai de sa bibliographie et de son histoire. 6 vols. New York, 1941.
Sart	Sarton, George. Introduction to the history of science. 3 vols. in 5. [Washington], I 1927; II 1931, 1931; III 1947, 1948.
Schramm	Schramm, Albert. Die Bilderschmuck der Frühdrucke, fortgeführt von der Kommission für den Gesamtkatalog der Wiegendrucke. 23 vols. Leipzig, 1920–43.
Schullian	Schullian, Dorothy M. A Catalogue of incunabula . . . in the Army Medical Library . . . New York [1950]. [A collection now in the National Library of Medicine at Bethesda, Maryland.]
Stegemann	Stegemann, Viktor. [*See below under*: Wehmer.]
Stevenson	Stevenson, Allan. The problem of the *Missale speciale*. London, 1967.
Stevenson-Briquet	Briquet, C. M. Les Filigranes [1907] . . . Amsterdam, 1968. [With introduction by Allan Stevenson.]
Stillw(AIS)	Stillwell, Margaret B. The awakening interest in science during the first century of printing, 1450–1550: An annotated checklist of first editions . . . Astronomy, Mathematics, Medicine, Natural Science, Physics, Technology, New York, 1970. (The Bibliographical Society of America.)
Stillw(G &C)	Stillwell, Margaret B. Gutenberg and the Catholicon of 1460 . . . New York, 1936. (With Latin texts and English translations of the tributes to Gutenberg in the printed books of the fifteenth century, 1468–1499.)
Stillwell	Stillwell, Margaret B. Incunabula in American libraries: A second census of fifteenth-century books owned in the United States, Mexico, and Canada. New York, 1940. (The Bibliographical Society of America.) [*Its numbers are also cited in the Third Census, 1964—cf: Goff.*]
Thorn(HM)	Thorndike, Lynn. History of magic and experimental science. 8 vols. New York, 1923–1958.

Voull(K)	Voulliéme, E. Der Buchdruck Kölns bis zum Ende des fünfzehnten Jahrhunderts, Bonn, 1903 (Gesellschaft für Rheinische Geschichtskunde, XXIV).
Wehmer	Wehmer, Carl. Mainzer Probedrucke in der Type des sogenannten astronomischen Kalenders für 1448. Ein Beitrag zur Gutenbergforschung. Mit einer Untersuchung: Der astronomische Kalender ein Planetentafel für Laienastrologen, von Viktor Stegemann. München, 1948.
Zedler	Zedler, G. Die Bamberger Pfisterdrucke und die 36-zeilige Bibel. Mainz, 1911. (Gutenberg-Gesellschaft. *Veröffentlichungen* X, XI.)

Symbols and Terms

★	An asterisk in the references (*Ref*:) indicates that the work designated by Hain was seen by him in Munich.
°	A symbol which, when used as an exponent and as part of a Latin abbreviation, indicates format, as — f°, *folio*; 4°, *quarto*; 8°, *octavo*; 12°, *duodecimo*.
——	A long dash in the title indicates the repetition of a title, or of a phrase having a corresponding position in the preceding title or edition.
[ ]	*In the imprint*, square brackets enclosing place, printer or date indicate that the data has been supplied, and is from some source other than the colophon, printer's device, or definite information within the work itself.
[ ]	*In the notation*, square brackets are used to indicate that, because of a change in date assignment, a work formerly assigned to an early date or period no longer comes within the scope of the present volume. [*See* Supplementary Sections: Undated Imprints currently unassigned, or re-assigned to 1470 or later.]
[ ]	*When enclosing an initial letter*, square brackets indicate that in the original type-setting space was left by the compositor for the insertion of a hand-wrought initial.

Abp.	Archbishop.
Add:	A note listing additional titles within a work or compilation; added entries.
Bdsde.	Broadside.
Blockbooks	Although contemporary with fifteenth-century books printed mechanically with *movable* metal types, the so-called blockbooks common to the

same period are of an entirely different genus. They belong to a small and self-contained discipline, a department of bibliography, the components of which are distinguished from printed books by a modifying prefix—as *xylographic-books* or *blockbooks*, meaning that their texts and illustrations were impressed by friction from carved wooden blocks, a full page at an impression or a considerable portion thereof.

Books	Although the term *book* has many applications, it is here used in the bibliographical sense of texts reproduced mechanically by movable metal types, the invention of which five hundred years ago marks the beginning of books as we know them and the starting point of bibliography itself. [*See also under: Blockbooks.*]
Bp.	Bishop.
BPubL	Boston Public Library, Boston, Massachusetts.
c.	*Circa*, about.
Comm:	Commentator(s).
Cop:	A note listing registered copies of the work or edition cited.
Costeriana	A term applied to a group of early pieces assigned to the Low Countries but unknown as to place, printer, or date; assigned at one time to the press of Lourenz Janszoon Coster at Haarlem. (*See* Appendix B.)
d.	Deceased.
Ed:	Edited by.
ELDML	Edward Laurence Doheny Memorial Library, Camarillo, California.
eponymous	In bibliographical usage, the term *eponymous press* is used to denote the press around which certain otherwise unidentifiable imprints have come to be grouped as a means of classification. Applicable only to the imprint of the work about which other works of the same typographical identity are grouped.
extant	Registered; known to be in existence at the present or a given time.
Fac:	A note citing a facsimile or reproductions of the work cited, in whole or in part.
ff, fol	Leaves or leaf.
fl.	Flourished; known to have been living at or about a given period, preferably an author's creative years.
frag	A fragment.
G, Goth ch.	In Gothic type or characters.
Issue	A term used for a book in which an important or considerable portion has been deliberately reset or altered. Applied as a median between a variant issue in which only a few points have been altered, and a new edition in which the text has been completely reset.

Abbreviations, Symbols, and Terms

Label-title	A caption printed on a preliminary leaf or page without other text or the printer's imprint.
LC	Library of Congress, Washington, D.C.
ll	lines to the page.
MFArt	Museum of Fine Arts, Boston, Massachusetts.
Mon:	A note citing a monograph on the work cited, or a section or article relative to it.
n	An annotation.
NYPL	New York Public Library, New York.
PML	Pierpont Morgan Library, New York.
Pont. Max.	Pontifex Maximus.
Prototypography	A term sometimes applied to early imprints assigned to the Low Countries; originally called Costeriana. (*See* Appendix B.)
Pseudo-	An attribution open to question; spurious.
publ	Publisher.
"published"	A term employed by medievalists with regard to manuscripts that were read before a scholarly or professional group—as *Papers* are read today before a learned society.
Ref:	A note citing bibliographical references.
rom, roman	A typographical term indicating so-called Roman type; a letter-design based on Roman inscriptions.
Scheide	Scheide Library (collection of John H. Scheide), Princeton, New Jersey.
Separate	An edition issued independently of other works; an excerpt; not in itself a part of a compilation of titles.
Sig	Signature; one of the series of folded sheets laid together so that they may be sewed to the bands of a binding. Signatures are frequently lettered and numbered in the lower margin of the first leaves of a gathering, but not on their conjugates. When citing a given reference on a conjugate, the letter and number are supplied in brackets.
[Sine nota]	Without statement of place, printer, or date within the work, and as yet unidentified and unassigned.
St.	Saint.
state	A term used comparatively to designate a type-font which, although ostensibly the same as another, shows by slight variations that the type has been recast, or that new sorts have been added or previous sorts discarded. When the recast letters indicate improvement, a basis for chronology is thus established.
Tr:	Translator(s).

unique	The only copy on record today.
var, variant	A copy which, although ostensibly the same as a given edition, is slightly different in some portion of its type-setting or text.
v., vol.	Volume(s).
Xylography	(*See above, under: Blockbooks.*)
Zel group	As the majority of the books printed at Cologne by Ulrich Zel are undated, their sequence presents a special problem. The solution introduced by Proctor has been elegantly presented in BMC by taking note of the progressive replacing of the letters "h" and "T"; the gradual introduction of type cast on a smaller base; and improvement in the registering or holding the paper in place, as shown by the resulting pinholes. It has thus proved possible to group the books in an acceptable and more or less chronological system, *i.e.*, Group A) Quartos wholly or mainly in type 96, with the *earlier h and T* and *four pinholes;* B) Quartos wholly or mainly in type 96 *recast* (96/99), with the *earlier h and T* and *four pinholes;* C:1) Quartos showing the *earlier T* and *earlier or later h* wholly or mainly in type 96 *recast*, but with *two pinholes;* C:2) later imprints with *no pinholes.* [It is on the basis of this system, that Zel's undated imprints are designated herein as groups A, B, C:1 or C:2.]

Books and Broadsides
1450 to 1470

A Chronological Checklist

Books and Broadsides
1450 to 1470

1450

BIBLIA LATINA (known as the 42-line Bible or the Gutenberg Bible).

1 —— [Mainz: Printer of the 42-line Bible (Johann Gutenberg and Associates), *c.* 1450–1455; not after August 1456.] f°.

> *Ref*: GW 4201; H *3031; BMC I 17; DeR(M) 34; Stillwell B460; Goff B-526.
>
> *N.B*: First issue, 40-, 41-, 42-lines to the column; second issue, 42-lines throughout. First issue with printing in red on 1ᵃ, 4ᵃ, 129ᵃ, 129ᵇ (the two main divisions of vol. 1). In two copies (Munich, Vienna) a 4-leaf table of rubrics is included. Presumed to have been on the press in the early years of the 1450s. According to the *Chronicle* printed at Cologne in 1499 (Goff C-476), printing began in 1450 after a decade of experimentation, "and the first book to be printed was the Bible in Latin." Completed before midsummer 1456, since in a copy in two volumes at the Bibliothèque Nationale in Paris a contemporary note states that Heinrich Cremer, Vicar of St. Stephans-Stift at Mainz, had completed the rubricating and binding of these volumes in August 1456, the first volume being dated 24 August and the second, 15 August of that year.
>
> *Mon*: SCHWENKE, P. *Zweiundvierzigzeilige Bibel*, Leipzig, 1923. LAZARE, E. *The Gutenberg Bible. A new census* (in the 1956 *Antiquarian Bookman*). NORMAN, D. C. *The 500th Anniversary Pictorial Census of the Gutenberg Bible*, Chicago, 1951.
>
> *Fac*: INSEL-VERLAG, Leipzig, 1913–1914, 2 v.; New York, 1960, 2 v.

1451/1452

SIBYLLENBUCH [*German*], *a fourteenth-century poem.*

2 —— [Mainz(?): in 36-line Bible type, *1st state, c.* 1451/1452.]

> *Ref*: DeR(M) 1; Ruppel (1939) 119–122, (1947) 116–118, *fac.*

3

1451—Sibyllenbuch (continued)

Cop: Known only through a fragment at the Gutenberg Museum in Mainz and comprising merely a section relating to the judgment of the world, for which reason it is sometimes referred to as the *Weltgericht*.

N.B: Until questioned by Dr. Carl Wehmer in 1948 in his *Mainzer Probedrucke*, this was believed to have been printed by Gutenberg in the 1440s, the earliest specimen of printing known. In Dr. Wehmer's system, it is assigned to the eponymous press of the so-called "Türkenkalender für 1455," printed presumably in December 1454 [no. 5, below].

As the result of a typographical analysis of the items within this group, Mr. George D. Painter, in his paper on *Gutenberg and the B36 Group: A Re-consideration*, notes "primitive imperfection" in the type which places the *Sibyllenbuch* as the earliest in the group. He further notes the presence [in a fluid state] of various Gutenbergian abutting-forms which appear in the 42-line or Gutenberg Bible—thus indicating that the B36 type was in existence "presumably before the B42 type was at the press." As the result of his analyses showing that the abutting forms in both fonts are of the Gutenbergian system, and because their production would have been prior to Gutenberg's partnership with Johann Fust, Mr. Painter submits that both fonts were produced by Gutenberg alone.

Fac: GUTENBERG GESELLSCHAFT. *Das Mainzer Fragment vom Weltgericht.* (*Veröffentlichungen*, III, 1904, pl. 1). McMURTRIE, D. C. *Some facts concerning the invention of printing*, Chicago, 1939, p. 13, gives reproductions of both sides of the fragment, and on p. 12 states that from the position of the watermark it has been possible to compute its probable position in the full sheet, and from the known text of the complete poem [1040 lines], it has been estimated that the book from which this fragment came was originally made up of thirty-seven leaves, or seventy-four pages, with twenty-eight type lines to the page. For complete facsimiles, see also ZEDLER in *Gutenberg Jahrbuch*, 1933, p. 26–30.

1452

DONATUS, Aelius, *fourth century*.

3   Ars minor (in 42-line Bible type, *early state*; *preceding the so-called first state?*). [Mainz: Johann Gutenberg, *c.* 1452.]

Ref: GW 8713; Stillwell D263; Goff D-318.
Cop: Scheide Collection (on deposit at Princeton University Library).
N.B: In 33-lines, on vellum. A fragment believed by Dr. Aloys Ruppel (*Johannes Gutenberg, sein Leben und sein Werk*, 1939, p. 156; 1947, p. 148) to be an experimental piece or proof, "etwa 1452," preceding the printing of the first forty pages of the "Gutenberg Bible." [For notes on other editions of Donatus in 42-line Bible type, see DONATUS [1468/69], nos. 133 and 134.]

DONATUS, Aelius, *fourth century*.

4   Ars minor. [Mainz: in 36-line Bible type, *1st state, c.* 1453–1454.]

Ref: GW 8676–8679; DeR(M) 2–4.

Cop: 27-line edition, known through fragments, on vellum: Darmstadt, Paris, and
Berlin (the so-called Heiligenstadt fragments).

N.B: A Latin grammar which served as a basic school-text for centuries and continued
in use long after printed copies became available. [For a note on the early text
in the recension of H. Keil (1864) and a nomalized text of the late Middle Ages
as re-constructed by P. Schwenke (1903), see GW VII col. 582–583.]

Such printed fragments as have survived indicate that various undated and
unsigned editions were issued directly after the invention of printing. Consequently, an immense amount of study has been expended upon those of apparently early date—Schwenke, Zedler, and other scholars counting them as
experimental pieces produced in the 1440s.

As the result of typographical analyses, however, Dr. Carl Wehmer in his
Mainzer Probedrucke, 1948, has shown that the pieces in 36-line Bible type,
which had been assigned to the 1440s, were printed at Mainz by an anonymous
press in the 1450s. He found them typographically related to the so-called
Turkish calendar (no. 5, below), to which the presumably definite date of 1454 is
assignable, and placed the Donatuses at somewhat after that date, about 1457–
1459. Incidentally, because of the superior presswork of the "Gutenberg Bible"
over these small ephemeral pieces, he inferred they did not come from the same
hand.

Mr. George D. Painter, however, in his recent essay on *Gutenberg and the
B36 Group: A Re-consideration*—as the result of his study of abutting letters and
other typographical factors in conjunction with those employed in the "Gutenberg Bible"—submits that all of the pieces in 36-line Bible type, the Donatuses
included, belong to the Gutenbergian system. Taking the *Turkish calendar* as the
criterion, or focal point, he establishes a chronological sequence in the early
editions of Donatus, by means of the state or improvement shown in their type.
His typographical analysis indicates that the 27-line edition, as known through
the fragments cited above, is somewhat earlier than the *Turkish calendar* but of
later date than the *Sibyllenbuch* (no. 2, above), since the sorts as they recur are in
improved setting "presumably owing to a recast of the type, or even to an
improvement in the casting-mould."

According to Dr. Wehmer's monograph, p. 40–41, a fragment of a 27-line
edition at Cracow (GW 8675) appears to be in a later state of the 36-line Bible
type than the fragments entered here. [For this and other fragments assigned to
about 1458, see no. 23, below.]

Fac: BOGENG, G. A. E. *Geschichte der Buchdruckerkunst der Frühdruck*, Dresden,
1930, opp. p. 256. For complete facsimiles, see ZEDLER in GUTENBERG-
GESELLSCHAFT. *Veröffentlichungen*, XXIII, Taf. 1–6 (GW 8676, 8677, 8679);
and I, Taf. 2–3 (GW 8678).

EYN MANUNG DER CRISTENHEIT WIDDER DIE DURKEN (*the so-called* Turkish calendar for 1455) [*German; dialect of Mainz*].

5 —— [Mainz: Eponymous press, in 36-line Bible type, *1st state*, December 1454.] 6 ff.

> *Ref*: H *10741; DeR(M) 19.
>
> *Cop*: Munich, *unique* (stored at Wiesbaden during World War II; missing since 1945 —Wehmer, *Mainzer Probedrucker*, p. 13, footnote 1).
>
> *N.B*: A propaganda pamphlet in verse, in which the section for each month is addressed to some high potentate of Christendom, warning him of the peril of invasion by the Turks. The fact that news is mentioned of a repulse of the infidels at the Hungarian border, which reached Frankfurt on 6 December, 1454, occasions the assignment of this tract to the latter portion of the month. Having found similar characteristics in typographical analyses, Dr. Carl Wehmer in his re-assignment of early pieces in 36-line Bible type uses this "Türkenkalender für 1455" as a focal point in assembling the group of fragments of unknown origin, that hitherto were assigned to the 1440s.
>
> The tract is interestingly described by Dr. Aloys Ruppel, with reproductions, in his book on *Johannes Gutenberg, sein Leben und sein Werk*, 1939, p. 127–131. As Dr. Ruppel indicates, the characteristics of a calendar are subordinated to the purposes of propaganda; the monthly divisions are used as a device for addressing the heads of church and state. Interestingly enough, the watermark in the paper is of a Turkish head and turban—propaganda on a grand scale.
>
> *Mon*: MORI, Gustav. *Der Türken-Kalender für das Jahr 1455* (Gutenberg Gesellschaft, 1928).
>
> *Fac*: *Gutenbergs Türkenkalender für das Jahr 1455* (Gutenberg Gesellschaft, 1928). NEUHAUS, J. *Das erste gedruckte Buch Gutenbergs in deutscher Sprache.* Copenhagen, 1902 (complete facsimile). Also, RUPPEL, p. 128, 168; GELDNER, p. 22, Abb. 1.

[6] Missale abbreviatum. *See* Supplementary Section: *Undated Imprints currently unassigned, or re-assigned to 1470 or later.*

[7] Missale speciale. *See* Supplementary Section: *Undated imprints currently unassigned, or re-assigned to 1470 or later.*

NICOLAUS V, *Pont. Max.* (Tommaso Parentucelli), 1398–1455.

8 Indulgentia (*the 31-line Indulgence, with printed textual date 1454*). [Mainz(?): in two types, 164G and 96G (the former the 36-line Bible type, *1st state*), not after 22 October, 1454.] Bdsde.

Ref: GW 6556: 1–5; Einbl 482–485; DeR(M) 47–49.

Cop: Variant printings known through copies or fragments on vellum: I, at Berlin; II, at Hannover, Wolfenbüttel; III, at Braunschweig; IV, at Berlin, Paris, and elsewhere; V, at Braunschweig, Wolfenbüttel.

N.B: A certificate of indulgence granted to contributors to the war against the Turks and Saracens, and for the defense of Cyprus. Paulinus Chappe, *commissary*. It is noted in GW 6556:4 that a fragment has the date "22 October" written in the spaces left for inserting the day and month. The printed year of the issuance, which reads *Datum Anno dni Mccccliiii*, provides the earliest in the history of printing that is definitely known. For a lengthy discussion of the indulgences of 1454 and 1455 and of the abutting-letters and other typographical factors indicating that the type employed in the indulgences is of the Gutenbergian system, see George D. Painter's essay on *Gutenberg and the B36 Group: A Re-consideration*, 1970. According to Mr. Painter (*The Library*, series 5, XVIII, no. 2, June 1963, p. 148), "Examination of Zedler's facsimiles of the six issues of the 30-line edition and seven issues of the 31-line edition . . . shows that only a single edition of each, from a single setting of type, was printed, and that the differences, including the year-dates, are merely press-variants. The entire edition of each must have come from the presses within a few days in 1454, and the issues dated 1455 were evidently due to the realization that the demand for the *Indulgences* would continue into the following year." Since it is also possible to assume that the form was kept in stock, in anticipation of later use, the issues dated 1455 are here listed under the year printed upon them—see nos. 10 and 11.

Mon: PAULUS, N. *Geschichte des Ablasses im Mittelalter*, Paderborn, 1923, III, 198 ff. ZEDLER, G. *Die Mainzer Ablassbriefe der Jahre 1454 und 1455*, Mainz (GUTEN-BERG-GESELLSCHAFT. *Veröffentlichungen*, XII, XIII, 1913. Taf. X-XIII, XV).

9 —— (*the 30-line Indulgence, with printed textual date 1454*). [Mainz: in two types, 140G and 90G (the former a version of the 42-line Bible type), with Schoeffer(?) initial, 1454.] Bdsde.

Ref: GW 6555:1; Einbl 487; DeR(M) 51; Ruppel (1939) 161, (1947) 152.

Cop: John Rylands Library, Manchester, *on vellum, unique*.

N.B: A certificate of indulgence granted to contributors to the war against the Turks and Saracens, and for the defense of Cyprus. Paulinus Chappe, *commissary*. The year of issuance is printed as *Datu . . . Mccccliiii* [regarding which, see note under no. 8, above]. Purchased at Cologne on 27 February, 1455, with the printed date 1454 altered to correspond.

Fac: ZEDLER, G. *Die Mainzer Ablassbriefe der Jahre 1454 und 1455* (GUTENBERG-GESELLSCHAFT. *Veröffentlichungen*, XII, XIII, 1913. Taf, IV.) McMUR-TRIE, D. C. *Some Facts concerning the Invention of Printing*, Chicago, 1939, p. 20. GELDNER, Ferdinand. *Die deutschen Inkunabel Drucker*, Stuttgart, 1968, p. 22, Abb. 3.

NICOLAUS V, *Pont. Max.* (Tommaso Parentucelli), 1398–1455.

10   Indulgentia (*the 31-line Indulgence, with printed textual date 1455*). [Mainz(?): in two types, 164G and 96G, the former the 36-line Bible type, *1st state*, 1455 or earlier.] Bdsde.

    Ref: GW 6556:6–7; Einbl 486; DeR(M) 50; Stillwell N37; Goff N-48.
    Cop: Variants known through copies: VI, at Heidelberg; VII, at London (BMC I 15), Manchester, and elsewhere including copies in USA at PML, NewL, and Scheide (*on deposit at Princeton*). [For copies of earlier issues in this series, see under no. 8 above.]
    N.B: A certificate of indulgence granted to contributors to the war against the Turks and Saracens and for the defense of Cyprus. Paulinus Chappe, *commissary*. Line 20 reads: Datum . . . Mcccclv . . . The dates of issuance range from 7 March, 1455 to 30 April, 1455. In his essay on *Gutenberg and the B36 Group: A Reconsideration*, Mr. Painter submits that the indulgences of 1454 and 1455 are "press-variants" since, with the exception of the dates, the typographical setting is the same. In his belief, both issues were printed in 1454 [but see note under no. 8, above].
    Fac: *Zentralblatt für Bibliothekswesen* XXXVI, 1919, p. 176. GUTENBERG-GESELLSCHAFT. *Veröffentlichungen*, XII, XIII, 1913. Taf. XIV.

11   —— (*the 30-line Indulgence, with printed textual date 1455*). [Mainz: in two types, 140G and 90G (the former a version of the 42-line Bible type), with Schoeffer(?) initial, 1455 or earlier.] Bdsde.

    Ref: GW 6555:2–6; Einbl 488, 489; DeR(M) 52, 53.
    Cop: Variant printings known through copies on vellum: I, at Hannover; II, at Karlsruhe, Wolfenbüttel; III, at London (BMC I 17); IV, at Berlin; V, at Düsseldorf. [For a copy of an earlier issue in this series, see no. 9 above.]
    N.B: A certificate of indulgence granted to contributors to the war against the Turks and Saracens, and for the defense of Cyprus. Paulinus Chappe, *commissary*. Line 20 reads: Datu . . . Mcccclquito . . . The dates of issuance range from 5 March, 1455 to 30 April, 1455. [For a note regarding the date of printing, see under no. 8, above.] According to BMC I 16–17, the first ornamental "M" in the text appears in a 1485 *Indulgentia* printed by Peter Schoeffer.
    Fac: BRITISH MUSEUM. Facsimiles, 1897, no. 3. GUTENBERG-GESELL-SCHAFT. *Veröffentlichungen*, XII, XIII, 1913. Taf. V–IX.

PSALTER [*Latin*]: Cantica, *fragment*.

12   —— [Mainz: in 42-line Bible type, about 1455.]

    Ref: DeR(M) 35.
    Cop: Known only through one leaf on vellum, at the Bibliothèque Nationale in Paris.

N.B: Described by Dr. Aloys Ruppel in his *Johannes Gutenberg*, 1939, p. 77, 156; 1947, p. 65, 148. Discussed by Dr. Klaus Konzog in his *Eine Mitteilung über den 42-zeiligen Liturgischen Psalter* (p. 72–74 in *Gutenberg Jahrbuch*, 1956); with partial reproduction.

1456

CALENDAR for 1457 [*Latin*] (*frequently called the* Aderlasskalender or Laxierkalender).

13 —— [Mainz(?): 36-line Bible type, *1st state*, 1456.] Bdsde.

Ref: GW 1286; Einbl 114; DeR(M) 21; Stillw (AIS) 324.
Cop: Bibliothèque Nationale, Paris (*fragment*).
N.B: The first medical piece known to have been printed. A calendar giving conjunctions and oppositions, and auspicious days for blood-letting or administering laxatives.
Fac: GUTENBERG-GESELLSCHAFT. *Veröffentlichungen*. I. Taf. V.

CALIXTUS III, *Pont. Max.* (Alfonso de Borja), 1378–1458.

14 Bulla contra Turcos. [Mainz: 36-line Bible type, *2nd state*(?), after 29 June, 1456/57.]

Ref: Bühler (FCB) 23; Goff C-60.
Cop: Scheide Collection (on deposit at Princeton University Library).
Fac: BÜHLER, Curt F. *Fifteenth Century Books and the twentieth century: An address . . . and a catalogue of an exhibition . . . at The Grolier Club*. New York, 1952, pl. 1.

15 —— [*German*:] Die bulla widder die Turcken. [Mainz: 36-line Bible type, *2nd state*(?), after 29 June, 1456.] 4°.

Ref: GW 5916; DeR(M) 20; Ruppel (1939) 132–134, (1947) 127–129, *fac.*
Cop: Berlin.
Mon: Probably printed between 29 June, 1456 (a date derived from the text) and the end of the year—see Wehmer, p. 40.
Fac: SCHWENKE, Paul, and Hermann DEGERING, ed. *Die Türkenbulle Pabst Calixtus III*. Berlin, 1911.

1457

CISIOIANUS [*German*] (*from Cisio Janus*; *also called Cisianus*).

16 —— [Mainz: 36-line Bible type, *2nd state*(?), c. 1457.] Bdsde.

1457—Cisioianus (continued)

Ref: GW 7054; Einbl 494; DeR(M) 22.

Cop: University of Cambridge (Oates 18), *on vellum*.

N.B: A calendar listing days of the year as applicable to every year. Without symbols pertaining to the solar and lunar cycles, and therefore not a perpetual calendar in the full technical meaning of the term; in rhymed couplets as an aid to learning the calendar dates. *Text begins*: Das ist der Cisianus zu dutsche . . . Because of its reference to Saint Bilhilt of Mainz, it is presumable that the calendar was printed there.

Mon: HAEBLER, Konrad. *Le soi-disant Cisianus* . . . (in *La Bibliographe Moderne*, VI, 1902, p. 1 ff, 188.)

Fac: GUTENBERG-GESELLSCHAFT. *Veröffentlichungen*. II, 1903. Taf. II.

PRECATIO.

17   —— [Mainz: 36-line Bible type, *2nd state*(?), 1457/58 or earlier.] Bdsde.

Cop: Munich.

N.B: Described by Dr. Ruppel in his *Johannes Gutenberg, sein Leben und sein Werk*, 1947, p. 130–131, as "etwa 1456/57," with the added note, "Der Text stammt aus den Schriften des hl. Anselm: Liber meditatione et orationum. Med. IX. (MIGNE: *Patrologia latina* 158, col. 759.)" According to the Wehmer type analysis, the second state of the 36-line Bible type is not known before 1457.

PSALTERIUM ROMANUM cum canticis, hymnis.

18   —— [Mainz:] Johann Fust and Peter Schoeffer, 14 August, 1457.   f°.

Ref: H 13479; BMC I 18; L-H no. 1; DeR(M) 54; Goff P-1036 (*9 leaves in North America*).

Cop: *2 issues, a)* London, Manchester, Windsor, Paris, Darmstadt; *b)* Angers, Paris, Berlin, Vienna, Dresden [Wiesbaden].

N.B: The first book to state its date of printing and the first to give its producers' names. The first also to include a colophon, a printer's device, or multi-color printing. Reputed to be one of the most beautiful books in the world. With handsome calligraphic initials, metal engraved, and printed simultaneously with the text, in red and blue or with touches of mauve. A book so rare that, until a copy was recently acquired by the Scheide Library, there was none in the country.

Known in two issues, both of which are at the Bibliothèque Nationale: *a)* 143 leaves; *b)* with part of the 143 leaves reset and 32 leaves added [Vigils of the Dead, *etc.*] The Vienna copy bears the firm's printer's device, possibly added after the production of the 1462 Bible, in which it appears in all copies [see *Gutenberg Jahrbuch*, 1950, 134 ff; 1952, 44 ff; 1959, 213–14.]

According to BMC I 19, the *Psalter* is the one used "in all churches of the Roman rite, except those in which the Monastic *Psalter* was used, but by means of the blank spaces [purposely left in the printing of the text] the characteristic differences of the use of any church for which a copy was purchased could be inserted." In a copy of the first issue at the British Museum, for instance, the necessary manuscript insertions adapted that copy of the *Psalter* to the usage of Mainz.

Mon: MASSON, *Sir* Irvine. *The Mainz Psalters and Canon Missae 1457–1459.* London: The Bibliographical Society, 1954. Plates.

Fac: A complete reproduction of the Vienna copy, with commentaries by Dr. Aloys Ruppel and Dr. Otto Mazal, was published at Stuttgart in 1969.

RESPICE DOMINE.

19 —— [Mainz: 36-line Bible type, *2nd state*(?), *c.* 1457.] Bdsde. 21 ll.

Ref: Einbl 1051.
Cop: Munich (Universitätsbibliothek).
N.B: *Text begins*: [R]Espice dn̄e sancte pater de excelso habitaculo celorū . . .

ROME, CHURCH of. Cancellaria Apostolica.

20 Provinciale omnium ecclesiarum. [Mainz: 36-line Bible type, *2nd state*(?), *c.* 1457 or earlier].

Ref: Ruppel (1947) 129–130.
Cop: Kiev (Akademie der Wissenschaften).
N.B: Four double leaves. The watermarks are known in a manuscript dated 1456, and the type is that of *Die bulla widder die Turcken*, which is assigned to about that year (see no. 15, above).
Mon: RUPPEL, A. *Ein bisher unbekannter Gutenbergdruck aufgefunden: das Provinciale Romanum* (p. 77–80 in *Archiv für Buchgewerbe und Gebrauchsgraphik* LXXX 1943). SCHOLDERER, V. *A unique Provinciale at Kiev* (p. 425 in *The Book Collector*, Winter, 1959).
Fac: ZDANEVIČ, B. J., *ed. Provinciale Romanum. Nevidome vidannia Joganna Gutenberga* (*Unbekannter Druck v. Johannes Gutenberg*), Kiieve, 1941.

1458

BIBLIA, 40-line [*Latin*].

21 —— [Mainz: in 36-line Bible type, *2nd state*, *c.* 1458 or earlier.]

Cop: Fragment at Cracow.
N.B: Printed on a leaf from a fourteenth-century Mainz cloth-merchant's ledger. Probably not a fragment of a complete Bible, but a trial-setting abandoned because a 40-line page proved to be too large when set in this state of the 36-line Bible type. For a comparison of the text of this fragment with corresponding sections in the 36- and 42-line Bibles, see WEHMER, Carl. *Mainzer Probedrucke*, 1948, p. 17–24. As the text differs from both of these, it is suggested that

1458—Biblia (continued)

it may have been set from the manuscript used in composing the 36-line Bible, before the latter's text was taken from that of the 42-line Bible.

Fac: WEHMER, Taf. 5.

CANON MISSAE.

22 —— [Mainz: Johann Fust and Peter Schoeffer, 1458.] f°. 12 ff.

Ref: DeR(M) 61; Stillwell M626; Goff M-736.

Cop: Oxford, Vienna — ColUL (9 ff, *vellum*); LC (Rosenwald Coll.) (Fol. 3, *frag.*, *vellum*); NewL (1 leaf, *vellum*).

N.B: With Schoeffer initials in red and blue, and a handsome "T," reproduced in WINSHIP, G. P. *Printing in the fifteenth century*, 1940, p. 44. The fact that two of the printed initials in the *Canon* show damage which does not appear in those of the 1457 *Psalter* but is intensified in the 1459 *Psalter*, has led to the assignment of the *Canon* between their dates. For a discussion of this edition of the *Canon Missae*, its beauty and its rarity, see LEHMANN-HAUPT, H. *Peter Schoeffer*, 1950, p. 40, 46, 60, plate 4. The Library of Congress fragment is described in *The Library*, 5th ser. XII, 1957, p. 43-44.

Mon: TRONNIER, A. *Über Anschlussbuchstaben, Setzer und Drucker im . . . Canon Missae des Jahres* [1458] (p. 66-79 in *Gutenberg Jahrbuch*, 1944/49). MASSON, Sir Irvine. *The Mainz Psalters and Canon Missae 1457-1459*. London: The Bibliographical Society, 1954. f°. Plates.

Fac: GOTTSCHALK, Paul. *Die Buchkunst Gutenbergs und Schöffers*, Berlin, 1918, no. 5.

DONATUS, Aelius, *fourth century*.

23a Ars minor. [Mainz: in 36-line Bible type, *2nd state, c.* 1458 or earlier.]

Cop: 26-line edition: Berlin-Trier fragment (GW 8674); Cracow (GW 8675).

N.B: See above, under no. 4. For the relation of D26-Cracow (GW 8675) to D27-Cracow (no. 23b, below), see Wehmer p. 24-31.

Fac: GUTENBERG-GESELLSCHAFT. *Veröffentlichungen*. XXIII, Taf. 31-34.

23b —— [——].

Cop: 27-line edition: variant fragments at Cracow (Wehmer 24-31); London (GW 8682, BMC I 16); Mainz; and elsewhere.

N.B: See above, under no. 4. Presser, in his essay on *Weitere Donatfragmente in Gutenberg Museum zu Mainz. Ergänzung zu dem 1454 mitgeteilen Verzeichnis* (p. 54-58 in GUTENBERG JAHRBUCH, 1959) identifies the fragment of the 27-line Donatus at Mainz as being close to GW 8682. GW 8676-8687 registers fragments of 27-line editions of Donatus at Bamberg (1), Darmstadt (1), Karlsruhe (1), London (1), Paris (1), Munich (2), and Berlin (5). [For reproductions, see GUTENBERG-GESELLSCHAFT. *Veröffentlichungen*, vols. I or XXIII.]

23c —— [——].

> *Cop:* 28-line edition: known in fragments at Munich, Mainz, Augsburg (GW 8688–8890), and at Columbia University (GW 8689; Stillwell D261; Goff D-316).
>
> *N.B:* See above, under no. 4. Wehmer assigns the various pieces in this type to about 1457–1459. Painter places these editions of Donatus at about 1458 or earlier, and calls attention to the fact that GW 8674, 8675, and 8689 have virtually even line-endings.
>
> *Fac:* GUTENBERG-GESELLSCHAFT. *Veröffentlichungen.* XXIII, Taf. 13, 35.

23d —— [——].

> *Cop:* 30-line edition: fragments at Berlin, London, Oxford, Karlsruhe, Prague, Mainz, Leipzig, and Berlin (GW 8691, 8692, 8694–97).
>
> *N.B:* See above, under no. 4. A fragment, cited as GW 8693 and reproduced as plate 12 in GUTENBERG-GESELLSCHAFT. *Veröffentlichungen* XXIII, was recorded, in Stillwell D262 as in the estate of Mr. Alvin W. Krech of New York. It failed, however, to be re-reported to Goff and its present location is unknown. [*In all, GW 8674–8697 devotes twenty-four entries to undated Donatuses printed in 36-line Bible type which, as the result of typographical comparison are now assigned as prior but close to the printing of the 36-line Bible, c. 1459/60.*]

PLANET-TABLE (Planetentafel für Laienastrologen; *the formerly so-called "Calendar for 1448") [German].*

24 —— [Mainz: 36-line Bible type, *2nd state, 1458.*]

> *Ref:* GW 1285; DeR(M) 5; Einbl 113.
>
> *Cop:* Variant fragments at Wiesbaden and Cracow, probably separate editions.
>
> *N.B:* A planet-table; that is, an astrological chart of the positions of the planets in 1448, for domestic use in casting horoscopes. For many years, because this was mistaken for a *calendar* for 1448, its printing was assigned to 1447. But, according to Dr. Stegemann, a specialist in medieval astrology, a planet-table such as this may be used as a basis for computations during several decades. That the fragments are on vellum would indicate that the table was not intended for ephemeral use.
>
> The Cracow fragment, which is either a rough proof for the Wiesbaden fragment, or a separate edition, shows a transitional stage in certain of its characters appearing in early pages of the 36-line Bible [1459/61, *third state*], but not thereafter. It is for this reason that Dr. Wehmer placed the planet-table at about 1458—i.e., in advance of but close to the production of the 36-line Bible. [*For review, see* BÜHLER, C. F. (p. 85–86 in BIBLIOGRAPHICAL SOCIETY of AMERICA. *Papers.* 1949). SCHOLDERER, V. (p. 229–231 in his *Fifty essays in fifteenth- and sixteenth-century bibliography,* 1966).]
>
> *Mon:* STEGEMANN, Viktor. *Ein Untersuchung der astronomische Kalendar. Eine Planetentafel für Laienastrologen* (p. 45–54 in WEHMER, Carl. *Mainzer Probendrucke in der Type der sogenannten astronomischen Kalenders für 1448,* München, 1948).

1458—*Planet-Table* (*continued*)

Fac: The Cracow and part of the Wiesbaden fragments are reproduced in the Wehmer monograph. Reproductions of the Wiesbaden fragments in its several sections appear in BURGER and VOULLIÉME. *Monumenta Germaniae*, p. 184; and on p. 17 in McMURTRIE, D. C. *Some facts concerning the invention of printing*, Chicago, 1939.

1459

BIBLIA, 36-line [*Latin*] (*the so-called* 36-line Bible).

25 —— [Bamberg?: Eponymous press, 36-line Bible type, *3rd state*, 1459/60, not after 1461.] f°.

Ref: GW 4202; BMC I 16; DeR(M) 23; Stillwell B461; Goff B-527.

N.B: Comparative collation shows that—with the exception of the first few leaves (vol. I, 1–5a; vol. II, 1–2a), which were perhaps set from the manuscript used in the 40-line fragment (no. 21, above)—the text of this edition was set from that of the 42-line Bible, which was printed before August 1456. According to Dr. František Horak (p. 116 in his Pět století cĕského knihtisku, Prague 1968), a Czech physician named Pavel Zídek wrote in 1459 of having seen a printed book in Bamberg, which may have been the 36-line Bible. A fragment of the 36-line Bible was found in the account-book in the Abbey of St. Michael at Bamberg, the earliest entry in which is 1 March, 1460. And support for a terminal date derives from a rubricator's date of 1461 in a copy of the 36-line Bible at the Bibliothèque Nationale at Paris. [Stevenson-Briquet, p. *95, indicates that the paper was in use as early as about 1458.]

The printing of the Bible is assigned to Bamberg on the ground that it is on paper known to have been in use there (but not known at Mainz); that several copies are in characteristic Bamberg bindings; that fragments of the text have been found as padding in the bindings of other books printed at Bamberg; and that the original provenance of practically all of the known copies centered at Bamberg or its vicinity.

The B36 type, in the same state as that of the Bible but somewhat worn, was used by Albrecht Pfister at Bamberg in 1461 and 1462. Pfister, however, has been rather ruled out as a possible printer of the Bible, because of the hasty and amateurish presswork of the pieces known to have come from his press. Mr. George D. Painter in his paper on *Gutenberg and the B36 Group: A Re-consideration*, as the result of typographical analysis and collation, shows proof that the B36 type was cut and cast in accordance with the Gutenbergian system of abutting-letters, and therefore by Gutenberg.

[By way of hypothesis—Painter submits that everything in B36 type was produced by Gutenberg up to the time it passed into the hands of Pfister. But Geldner submits that Kefer, one of Gutenberg's workmen, may have gone with the type to Bamberg and printed the Bible there. To this hypothesis Mr. Painter adds the ingenious suggestion that Gutenberg, while continuing to work in

Mainz, may have "shuttled to and fro" in order to oversee the job. Thus Gutenberg, while busy with the cutting and casting of the type for the *Catholicon* at Mainz, could have kept an eye on the printing of the 36-line Bible at Bamberg and Mr. Painter (who would like to hold Gutenberg responsible for both the Bible and the *Catholicon*) could have his heart's desire. The cutting and casting of type, however, is an entirely separate function from that of setting type and printing the pages of text. Whether or not Gutenberg performed both functions for both books is a question that has not as yet been fully answered.]

Mon: ZEDLER, G. *Die Bamberger Pfisterdrucke und die 36zeilige Bibel* (GUTENBERG-GESELLSCHAFT. *Veröffentlichungen*, X, XI, 1911). WEHMER, C. *Mainzer Probedrucke*, München, 1948, p. 19–24. GELDNER, F. *Het Heinrich Kefer aus Mainz die 36zeilige Bibel gedruckt?* (p. 100–110 in *Gutenberg-Jahrbuch* 1950); *Die Buchdruckekunst im alten Bamberg*, Bamberg, 1964, p. 17–23; *Die deutschen Inkunabeldrucker*, Stuttgart, 1968. DOLD, Alban. *Die Beweisstücke für die Priorität der B42 vor der B36 in Lichtbild dargeboten und kurz erläutert* (p. 40–51 in *Gutenberg-Jahrbuch* 1951). DRESSLER, A. *Hat Gutenberg in Bamberg die 36zeilige Bibel gedruckt?* (p. 553–556, 610–622, 701–704 in *Börsenblatt für den deutschen Buchhandel* 1954 X; *Nachtrag* 1955 XI). SCHNEIDER, Heinrich. *Der Text der 36zeiligen und des Probedrucke von circa 1457* (p. 57–69 in *Gutenberg-Jahrbuch* 1955). RASARIVO, Raúl Mario. *Der goldene Modul der 36zeiligen Bibel. Die Entdeckung eines Werkstattgeheimnisses Johann Gutenberg*, with geometrical analyses of 2 pages of the Bible (p. 70–74 in *Gutenberg-Jahrbuch* 1955). PAINTER, G. D. *Gutenberg and the B36 Group: A Re-consideration* (Scholderer *Festschrift*. Dennis E. Rhodes, *ed.* Mainz, 1970). [See also RANDALL, D. A. (p. 173–174 in BIBLIOGRAPHICAL SOCIETY of AMERICA, *Papers*, 56, 1962).]

DURAND, Guillaume (Durandus; Guillelmus Duranti), *Bp. of Mende*, 1237–1296.

26 Rationale divinorum officiorum. [Mainz:] Johann Fust and Peter Schoeffer, *clericus*, 6 October, 1459. f°.

Ref: GW 9101; HR 6471; BMC I 20; DeR(M) 65; Stillwell D328; Goff D-403.
N.B: A treatise in eight books relating to church symbolism in vestments, architecture, etc. In a new, small type set in double columns, with Schoeffer initials in red and blue. The term, *clericus*, in the colophon indicates the status of Peter Schoeffer in 1459. Known in several variants. (The author—Bishop of Mende, papal regent, and a specialist in civil and canon law—is not to be confused with his nephew of the same name, *d.* 1330, who at one time was also Bishop of Mende.)
Fac: LEHMANN-HAUPT, H. *Peter Schoeffer*, 1950, plate 5.

PSALTERIUM BENEDICTINUM (Congregationis Bursefeldensis).

27 —— [Mainz:] Johann Fust and Peter Schoeffer, 29 August, 1459. f°.

Ref: BMC I xxiv, 19; DeR(M) 55; Stillwell P970; Goff P-1062.

1459—Psalterium Benedictinum (continued)

> *N.B*: Known also as the *Observantia per Germaniam*. Issued in accordance with the Reformed Monastic Breviary of the Union of Bursfeld. Presumably printed for the use of the Benedictine Monastery of St. Jacob at Mainz, since the phrase "ad laudem dei ac honorem Sancti Jacobi" occurs in the colophon.
>
> *Mon*: GELDNER, F. *Um das Psalterium Benedictinum von 1459* (p. 71–83 in *Gutenberg Jahrbuch*, 1954). MASSON, *Sir* Irvine. *The Mainz Psalters and Canon Missae, 1457–1459*. London: The Bibliographical Society, 1954.
>
> *Fac*: LEHMANN-HAUPT, H. *Peter Schoeffer*, Rochester, 1950, plates 1–3. WINSHIP, G. P. *Printing in the fifteenth century*, Philadelphia, 1940, p. 44.

THOMAS AQUINAS, *St.*, 1225–1274.

28   De articulis fidei et ecclesiae sacramentis. [Mainz: Printer of the Balbi *Catholicon* (Johann Gutenberg?), 1459/60?] 4°.

> *Ref*: DeR(M) 92; Ruppel (1939) 184, (1947) 173; Stillwell T248; Goff T-273.
>
> *N.B*: Known in two issues, of 34- and 36-lines respectively. This first edition of any of the writings of Thomas Aquinas is listed on Schoeffer's advertisement of 1469/70, where it is stated that all titles entered there were printed at Mainz.

1460

ACKERMANN von Böhmen [*German*].

29   —— [Bamberg: Albrecht Pfister, 36-line Bible type, *3rd state, c.* 1460 or earlier.] f°.

> *Ref*: GW 193; DeR(M) 26; Schramm I p. 1, 7; Goff A-39.
>
> *N.B*: *Text begins*: An dem buchlein ist beschriben ein krig waṅ einer dem sein libes weib gestorben ist schildtet den todt ... Attributed to Johannes von Saaz of Prague, whose wife had died in 1400.
>
> Because of inept technique, this is believed to be the earliest of the group of illustrated books published by Albrecht Pfister at Bamberg, which show improved technique in the course of the series. Possibly the first book to contain woodcut illustrations. Known only in an imperfect copy at Wolfenbüttel.
>
> In some bibliographies this edition is assigned to 1458 on the ground that, since the next item in the Pfister series—Boner's *Der Edelstein* of February 1461—contains close to a hundred separate woodcuts, adequate time should be allowed for their production, between the two imprints. But from 1458 to 1461 as a time allowance seems rather excessive. The wood-engraver who produced the *Edelstein* cuts, and the journeyman printer who produced the Ackermann, presumably worked independently. Even if they were one and the same person, it would seem from the simplicity of the illustrations in the *Edelstein* and the directness of approach in their conception, that carving the woodblocks for the cuts could not have been too time-consuming. The year 1460, therefore, seems a more reasonable assignment, and it has the advantage of bringing the Ackermann nearer to the 1461–1462 group to which it belongs and of placing it after

the completion of the 36-line Bible, which presumably preceded the founding of Pfister's office.

Mon: ZEDLER, G. *Die Bamberger Pfisterdrucke* (GUTENBERG- GESELLSCHAFT. *Veröffentlichungen*, X, XI, 1911). With reproductions. Reviewed by V. Scholderer in *The Library*. Ser. III, vol. III, 1912, p. 230–236.

Fac: Leipzig: Insel Verlag, 1919 (Ed: Alois Bernt).

BALBI, Giovanni (Johannes Balbus), *d.* 1298.

30   Catholicon. Mainz: [Eponymous press (Johann Gutenberg ?)] 1460. f°.

Ref: GW 3182; DeR(M) 90; Ruppel (1939) 175–183, (1947) 164–172; Stillwell B19; Goff B-20.

N.B: An edition was issued by Günther Zainer at Augsburg, 30 April 1469 (Goff B-21); and two editions were brought out at Strasbourg by the R.-Printer (Adolf Rusch) about 1470 (Goff B-22, -23). Twenty-four editions of this imposing glossary of the Latin language were published before 1501—in Germany (8), France (10), and Italy (6).

Mon: STILLWELL, M. B. *Gutenberg and the Catholicon of 1460*, New York, 1936, with a census of copies and translations in English of the tributes to Gutenberg in the printed books of the fifteenth century. GELDNER, Ferdinand. *Das "Catholicon" des Johannes Balbus im ältesten Buchdruck* (p. 90–98 in OHLY, K. and KRIEG, W., *ed. Aus der Welt des Bibliothekars: Festschrift für Rudolf Juchhoff*. Cologne [1961]).

BENEDICTUS XII, *Pont. Max.* (Jacques Fournier), *d.* 1342.

31   *Bulla*: Ad regimen universalis ecclesiae. (*Issued with* CLEMENS V, *Pont. Max.* Constitutiones. [Mainz:] Johann Fust and Peter Schoeffer, 25 June 1460—see no. 32, below.)

CLEMENS V, *Pont. Max.* (Bertrand de Goth, Raimundus Bertrandi del Goth), *c.* 1264–1314.

32   Constitutiones (Comm: Joannes Andreae (Giovanni d'Andrea), *jurist*, *c.* 1270–1348). *Bulla*: Exivi de paradiso [Rule of St. Francis]. [Mainz:] Johann Fust and Peter Schoeffer, 25 June, 1460. f°.

Add: JOANNES XXII, *Pont. Max.*, *d.* 1334. *Bulla*: Constitucio̅ execrabilis. BENE-DICTUS XII, *Pont. Max.*, *d.* 1342. *Bulla*: Ad regimen universalis ecclesiae.

Ref: GW 7077; H 5410; BMC I 20; DeR(M) 66; L-H 4; LC(LJRCat) 24; Stillwell C647; Goff C-710.

N.B: The first edition of a book of Canon Law. All extant copies printed on vellum. Two pinholes in the lower margin. The volume consists mainly of the so-called Clementine laws "published" in 1317, which followed the 1298 *Liber Sextus Decretalium* of Bonifacius VIII (see no. 71 below). The inclusion of items by Benedictus XII and Joannes XXII—the earliest instance of a printed compilation

1460—Clemens V. (continued)

—makes the present volume reminiscent of the three earliest Avignonese popes. Clemens V and especially Joannes XXII sought increased independence and power for the Church through the acquisition of vast wealth. And through the development of the Curia into a highly organized bureaucracy, they greatly increased papal control within the Church. Benedictus XII in his monastic constitution sought clerical reforms largely through re-enactment and confirmation of former regulations.

Following the manuscript tradition, the commentary is printed around the *Constitutiones* like a border (the Commentary, in 1459 Durand type; the text, in type later used for the 1462 Bible).

33a Exivi de paradiso [Rule of St. Francis]. [Mainz:] Johann Fust and Peter Schoeffer, 25 June, 1460—see no. 32, above.

DONATUS, Aelius, *fourth century.*

33b Ars minor. [Mainz (or Bamberg?): in 36-line Bible type, *2nd or 3rd state, n.d.*]

> *N.B:* Although the fragments of this 28-line edition were assigned by Dr. Aloys Ruppel to [Bamberg, *c.* 1460], as an early product of Albrecht Pfister's press (*Johannes Gutenberg*, 1939, p. 140; 1947, p. 136), more recent research assigns it to Mainz prior to the printing of the 36-line Bible. [See under 1458, no. 23c, above.]

JOANNES XXII, *Pont. Max.* (Jacques d'Euse), 1244–1334.

34 Bulla: Constitutio Execrabilis. (*Issued with* CLEMENS V, *Pont. Max.* Constitutiones. [Mainz:] Johann Fust and Peter Schoeffer, 25 June, 1460—see no. 32, above.)

MATTHIAS de Cracovia, *Bp. of Worms, c.* 1335–1410.

35 Dialogus rationis et conscientiae de frequenti usu communionis. [Mainz: in the type of the 1460 *Catholicon* (Johann Gutenberg?), 1460?] 4°.

> *Ref:* H*5803; BMC I 40; Ruppel (1939) 183, (1947) 172; AmBCat 1; DeR(M) 91; Stillwell M323; Goff M-367.
> *N.B:* Either leading was set between the lines (in that event, the first known), or the type was cast on a larger body than that of the *Catholicon.*

1461

ALMANACH für Wien, 1462 [*German*].

36 —— [Germany, Vienna(?): n. pr., 1461.] Bdsde. 52 ll.

Ref: GW 1287; Einbl 115; Geldner 294; Stillw (AIS) 267.

N.B: *Text begins* [] ye gulden czal . . . Known only in a copy at Donaueschingen. An almanac reckoned from the meridian of Vienna, thus suggesting Vienna as a possible place for its printing. Refers to auspicious times for blood-letting. Although Ulrich Han has been suggested as printer, Geldner does not consider him a likely candidate. The minuscules are the same as those in the *Passione di Cristo* (no. 57, below).

Fac: HEITZ-HAEBLER. *Hundert Kalender-Inkunabeln*, no. 2. Strassburg, 1905. Taf. 2.

AUGUSTINUS, Aurelius, *St., Bp. of Hippo*, 354–430.

37   De vita christiana. [Mainz:] Johann Fust and Peter Schoeffer [*c.* 1461]. 4°.

Ref: GW 3037 (*Pseudo*); C 768; BMC I 20; DeR(M) 88; Stillwell A1205; Goff A-1354.

N.B: The copy in the Huntington Library contains the firm's printer's-mark, an emblem analogous to a signature; not found in other copies. From its relation to adjoining titles on Schoeffer's advertising-list of 1469/70, this tract would seem to have been issued early in the decade, a point that is supported by the position of hyphens outside of the page alignment, indicative of early origin.

BIBLIA, 49-lines [*Latin*].

38   —— [Strasbourg: Johann Mentelin, not after 1460/61.] f°.

Ref: GW 4203; H ★3033; BMC I 51; Stillwell B462; Goff B-528.

N.B: The copy at Freiburg im Breisgau has a rubricator's date, 1460 in vol. 1, and 1461 in vol. 2. Except for the appearance of Mentelin's name in the preface of a St. Augustine of 1466 (Goff A-1226), his early products are unsigned and are known through his later advertisements of stock. Because of its smaller type and frequent use of abbreviations, the text of this edition of the Bible is compressed into 854 pages, as against 1,286 in the 42-line Bible and 1,768 in the 36-line Bible. The question of space compression as exemplified by these editions is discussed, p. 23, 38–50, in WINSHIP, G. P. *Printing in the fifteenth century*, Philadelphia, 1940.

BONER, Ulrich, *fl.* 1350.

39   Der Edelstein [*German*]. Bamberg: [Albrecht Pfister, 36-line Bible type, *3rd state*] "An sant valenteins tag" (14 Feb.), 1461. f°.

Ref: GW 4839; Schramm I, p. 1–4.

N.B: The earliest *dated* book in German and the earliest *dated* instance of woodcut illustrations combined with printed text. A fourteenth-century fable; with 203 woodcut illustrations, including repeats. No. 2 in Zedler's analysis of early Bamberg prints. A copy at Wolfenbüttel, *unique*, is in a binding with arms of Napoleon I.

1461—Boner (continued)

Fac: Reproduced in part in GRAPHISCHE GESELLSCHAFT. I. *Ausserordentliche Veröffentlichung*. Berlin, 1908. LONE, E. M. *Some noteworthy firsts*, New York, 1930, p. 4. SCHRAMM I, pl. 8–111.

FRIEDRICH III, *Emperor*, 1415–1493.

40   *Manifesto*: [w]Ir friederich von gottis gnaden Romischer Keyser zu allen czitten . . . [Sanctioning the deposition of Diether von Isenberg from the Archbishopric of Mainz]. Graz, 8 August, 1461. [Mainz: Johann Fust and Peter Schoeffer 1461.] Bdsde. 28 ll.

Ref: Einbl 599; BMC I 21; L-H 6; DeR(M) 69.
N.B: In the type used in the Bible of 1462 (no. 51, below).

PIUS II, *Pont. Max.* (Eneas Sylvio Piccolomini), 1405–1464.

41   *Breve*: [P]Ius epūs . . . Adolpho de Nassau [Apostolic brief to Adolf II von Nassau sanctioning his election to the Archbishopric of Mainz]. Tivoli, 21 August, 1461. [Mainz: Johann Fust and Peter Schoeffer, 1461.] Bdsde. 27 ll.

Ref: Einbl 1194; BMC I 21; L-H 7; DeR(M) 72; Goff P-655.
Cop: Copies known at the British Museum and the Edward Laurence Doheny Memorial Library, Camarillo, California.

42   —— [*Variant issue.*] *Breve*: [P]Iūs Epūs . . . Adulpho de Nassau . . .

Ref: Einbl 1195; BMC I 22; L-H 8; DeR(M) 71.
Fac: ROSENTHAL, J., *publ. Incunabula typographica*, p. 142.

43   *Breve*: [P]Ius Epūs . . . Captio ecclesie Maguntiñ [Brief to the Cathedral Chapter in Mainz regarding the election of Adolf II von Nassau to the Archbishopric.] Tivoli, 21 August, 1461. [Mainz: Johann Fust and Peter Schoeffer, 1461.] Bdsde. 24 ll.

Ref: Einbl 1196; BMC I 22; L-H 9; DeR(M) 73.

44   *Breve*: [P]Ius Epūs . . . vniuersis Capitulis. Prepositis. Scolasticis . . . [Brief addressed to the clergy and civil officials of the diocese of Mainz, sanctioning the election of Adolf II von Nassau to the Archbishopric.] Tivoli, 21 August, 1461. [Mainz: Johann Fust and Peter Schoeffer, 1461.] Bdsde. 18 ll.

Ref: Einbl 1198; BMC I 22; L-H 11; DeR(M) 74.
Fac: ROSENTHAL, J., *publ. Incunabula typographica*, p. 143.

45 *Entry cancelled.*

46 *Bulla*: [P]Ius ep̄s ... In apl'ice sedis specula [concerning the deposition of Diether von Isenberg, Archbishop of Mainz]. Tivoli, 21 August, 1461. [Mainz: Johann Fust and Peter Schoeffer, 1461.] Bdsde. 87 ll.

    Ref: Einbl 1197; BMC I 21; L-H 10; DeR(M) 70.

47 *Bulla*: [P]Ius Epūs ... venerabilibz fratribz Archiep̄is Ep̄is et alÿs ... [announcing to the clergy and civil authorities of Germany that contributions to the crusade against the Turks would not be demanded without their consent]. Tivoli, 4 September, 1461. [Mainz: Johann Fust and Peter Schoeffer, 1461.] Bdsde. 28 ll.

    Ref: Einbl 1199; BMC I 22; L-H 12; DeR(M) 75.

48 Indulgentia, 1461 [for the benefit of the Church of St. Cyriakus at Neuhausen]. [Mainz: in the type of the 1460 *Catholicon*, 1461.] Bdsde. 15 ll.

    Ref: GW 76; Einbl 50; DeR(M) 94; Ruppel (1939) 184–185, (1947) 173–174.
    N.B: DeR(M) 94 refers to a copy owned by Count Alexis Razoumoffsky in 1810, but now lost. Known only through the facsimile noted below.
    Fac: GUTENBERG-GESELLSCHAFT. *Veröffentlichungen*. IV. Taf. 7.

49 —— 1461 [for the benefit of the Church of St. Cyriakus at Neuhausen]. [Mainz: Johann Fust and Peter Schoeffer, 1461.] Bdsde. 15 ll.

    Ref: GW 77; L-H 5; Einbl 51; DeR(M) 67(?).

1462

ADOLF II von Nassau, *Abp. of Mainz, d. 1475.*

50 *Manifesto*: [W]ijr haben vernūmē das Diether von Isenberg [*German*]. [Answer to accusations made by Diether von Isenberg.] [Mainz: Johann Fust and Peter Schoeffer, 1462.] Bdsde. 58 ll.

    Ref: GW 225; Einbl 87; BMC I 22; L-H 14; DeR(M) 76.

BIBLIA [*Latin*], (the so-called 1462 Bible).

51 —— Mainz: Johann Fust and Peter Schoeffer, *clericus*, "In vigilia assumptionis Mariae" (14 August), 1462. f°.

> *Ref*: GW 4204, *issues a, b*; BMC I 22; DeR(M) 79; L-H 16; Stillwell B463; Goff B-529.
>
> *N.B*: Printed in black and red, with initials printed in red and blue. Two issues known. Not usually designated by the number of lines to the page (48 lines), since unlike earlier Bibles this has a printed date by which it may be identified. Contains the printer's device in red and is the earliest book from this press said to contain the device in all copies. The term *clericus* in the colophon indicates the status of Peter Schoeffer in 1462.
>
> *Fac*: LEHMANN-HAUPT, H. *Peter Schoeffer*, 1950, plate 7.

BIBLIA PAUPERUM [*German*].

52 —— [Bamberg: Albrecht Pfister, in 36-line Bible type, *3rd state*, after May Day, 1462.] f°.

> *Ref*: GW 4325; Pell 2388; DeR(M) 30; Schramm I, p. 5, 7.
>
> *N.B*: The first printed edition of the *Poor Man's Bible*. A picture-book Bible with brief excerpts or captions in German indicating the text illustrated. The multitude of pictures was intended to make the story intelligible to the common man. Illustrated by 136 woodcuts, including repeats. No. 4 in Zedler's system of early Bamberg imprints. As the result of typographical analysis, this is rated as after Pfister's edition of the *Vier Historien* which was printed in 1462 "Nit lang nach sand walpurgen tag."
>
> *Fac*: GUTENBERG-GESELLSCHAFT. *Veröffentlichungen*. X, XI. Taf. 13, 14. GELDNER, p. 50. SCHRAMM I, pl. 167–268.

53 —— [*Latin*]. [Bamberg: Albrecht Pfister, in 36-line Bible type, *3rd state*, after May Day, 1462.] f°.

> *Ref*: GW 4326; DeR(M) 32; Schramm I, p. 7.
>
> *N.B*: The first printed edition of the *Poor Man's Bible* with Latin text. With 136 woodcuts, including repeats. No. 5 in Zedler's analysis of early Bamberg imprints.
>
> *Fac*: GUTENBERG-GESELLSCHAFT. *Veröffentlichungen*. X, XI. Taf. 15, 16. SCHRAMM I, pl. 269–305.

BONER, Ulrich, *fl.* 1350.

54 Der Edelstein [*German*]. [Bamberg: Albrecht Pfister, in 36-line Bible type, *3rd state*, after May Day 1462.] f°. 28 ll.

> *Ref*: GW 4840; DeR(M) 26; Schramm I, p. 1, 7.
>
> *Cop*: Berlin, *unique*.
>
> *N.B*: Second edition. With 206 woodcut illustrations, including repeats. No. 8 in Zedler's analysis of early Bamberg imprints.
>
> *Fac*: GRAPHISCHE GESELLSCHAFT. *Ausserordentliche Veröffentlichung*. I. Berlin, 1908. SCHRAMM I, pl. 8–111 [1464].

DIETHER von Isenberg, *Abp. of Mainz, c.* 1412–1482.

55   *Appelatio*: [B]Eatissime pater . . . [Appeal to Pope Pius II regarding tenure of the Archbishopric]. [Mainz: Johann Fust and Peter Schoeffer, before 14 October 1462.] Bdsde. 31 ll.

    Ref: GW 8339; Einbl 515; L-H 17; DeR(M) 77 [August *or* September, 1462].
    N.B: The terminal date of 14 October, 1462 is fixed by a letter of that date at Frankfurt, in which this broadside is mentioned.

56   *Manifesto*: [A]llen vnd iglichen fursten, Grauen. herren, prelaten . . . In was staidts wirden oder wesens sie sin . . . [Manifest against Adolf von Nassau]. Höchst, 30 March, 1462. [Mainz: Johann Fust and Peter Schoeffer, 1462.] Bdsde. 106 ll.

    Ref: GW 8338; Einbl 514; L-H 15; DeR(M) 78.

PASSIONE DI CRISTO (*Italian version of the 'Leiden Christi' frequently printed in Germany*).

57   —— [S. Germany?: n.p., about 1462?]

    Ref: Geldner p. 292–3; Stillwell P128; Goff P-147.
    N.B: Illustrated with 20 metalcuts. Variously assigned to Germany or Italy, 1462–1477. According to Dr. Konrad Haebler in his *Die italienischen Fragmente vom Leiden Christi*, Munich, 1927, this apparently unique fragment was probably printed in Italy. But Dr. Victor Scholderer in his *Printers and readers in Italy in the fifteenth century* (p. 202 in his *Fifty essays in fifteenth- and sixteenth-century bibliography*, 1966), submits that it was printed in Germany for the Italian market, to be hawked about by colporteurs. Dr. Donati sees it not as a *Passio*, but as a popular collection of prayers inspired by the Passion; based on a Latin text and assignable to the press of Damianus de Moyllis at Padua in 1477 or earlier. Dr. R. Ridolph, on the other hand, accepts an early date and considers the *Passione* printed in Germany for the Italian trade (p. 41 in his *La stampa in Firenze nel secolo XV*, Firenze, 1958). Dr. Geldner identifies the *Passione* as from the same press as the *Sieben Freuden Mariae* [Mainz?: Johann Neumeister?, *c.* 1460/64], and gives two pages of the latter in reproduction. The minuscules identify with those in the *Almanach für Wien, 1462* (no. 36, above).
    Mon: DONATI, Lamberti. *Passio Domini nostri Iesu Christi. Frammento tipografico della Biblioteca Parsoniana* (p. 181–215 in *Bibliofilia*, LVI, 1954).

PIUS II, *Pont. Max.* (Eneas Sylvio Piccolomini), 1405–1464.

58a   Indulgentia, 1462 [for the benefit of the Church of St. Cyriakus at Neuhausen. Formula for women]. [Mainz: Johann Fust and Peter Schoeffer, 1462.] Bdsde. 16 ll.

> *Ref*: GW 79; Einbl 53; L-H 13; DeR(M) 68 (*facsimile*).
> *N.B*: With initial "K."
> *Fac*: *Zeitschrift für Bücherfreunde*. N.F. III, p. 132.

58b   —— [Mainz: in the type of the 1460 *Catholicon*, before 10 April 1462.]
Bdsde. 18 ll.

> *Ref*: GW 78; Einbl 52; Ruppel (1939) 184–185, (1947) 173–174, *fac*.
> *N.B*: Stuttgart copy, *unique*, with day and month inserted in a contemporary hand.
> *Fac*: *Zeitschrift für Bücherfreunde*. N.F. III, p. 67.

SIEBEN FREUDEN MARIAE.

59   —— [*German*]. [S. Germany?: Printer of the 'Passione di Cristo,' about
1462?] sm. 8°.

> *Ref*: Geldner, p. 292–3, with reproduction of 2 pages; Schreiber 4570a.
> *N.B*: Illustrated with 8 metalcuts. Geldner suggests that this was issued with the
> *Passione di Cristo*, possibly at Mainz by Johann Neumeister. *See under no. 57,*
> *above.*
> *Fac*: HAEBLER, Konrad. *Die italienischen Fragmente vom Leiden Christi*. Munich,
> 1927, pl. IV.

VIER HISTORIEN von Joseph, Daniel, Judith, und Hester [*German*].

60   —— Bamberg: Albrecht Pfister, [*c.* May Day] 1462. f°.

> *Ref*: DeR(M) 27; Schramm I, p. 7.
> *N.B*: With 61 woodcuts, including repeats. No. 3 in Zedler's analysis of early
> Bamberg imprints. With colophon reading: Dē puchlein ist sein ende gebē.
> Czu Bambergk in der selbē stat. Das albrecht pfister gedrucket hat Do mā zalt
> tausent vn̄ vier hūdert iar. Im zweiundsechzigstē das ist war. Nit lang nach sand
> walpurgen tag.
> *Fac*: SCHRAMM I, pl. 114–166.

1463

ACKERMANN von Böhmen.

61   —— [Bamberg: Albrecht Pfister, in 36-line Bible type, *3rd state, c.* 1463.]
f°.

> *Ref*: GW 194; DeR(M) 29; Schramm I, p. 7; Goff A-39.
> *N.B*: Attributed to Johannes von Saaz of Prague. Second edition. With 5 woodcuts.
> No. 6 in Zedler's analysis of early Bamberg imprints.

Fac: BERNT, Alois, *ed.* Leipzig, Insel-Verlag, 1919. GUTENBERG-GESELL-SCHAFT. *Veröffentlichungen*. X, XI. Taf. 19, 20.

BIBLIA PAUPERUM [*German*].

62 —— [Bamberg: Albrecht Pfister, in 36-line Bible type, *3rd state, c.* 1463.] f°.

Ref: GW 4327; Pell 2387; Schramm I, p. 5, 7.
N.B: Second edition. With 176 woodcuts, including repeats. No. 7 in Zedler's analysis of early Bamberg imprints. First issued by this press, after May Day, 1462.
Fac: GUTENBERG-GESELLSCHAFT. *Veröffentlichungen*. X, XI. Taf. 17, 18. SCHRAMM I, pl. 167–268.

JACOBUS de Theramo (Jacopo Palladini de Teramo), *Abp. of Taranto*, 1350–1417.

63 Processus Belial, seu Consolatio peccatorum [*German*]. Bamberg: Albrecht Pfister [in 36-line Bible type, *3rd state, c.* 1463.] f°.

Ref: Cop 5785; DeR(M) 33.
N.B: A fable written according to Canon Law and purporting to record the trial of Christ before Solomon, on the Devil's charge that He had been stealing souls through redemption. No. 9 in Zedler's analysis of early Bamberg imprints. The only one of the Pfister series not having illustrations. [Stevenson-Briquet, p. ★95, indicates that the paper may have been in use as early as about 1460.]

PIUS II, *Pont. Max.* (Eneas Sylvio Piccolomini), 1405–1464.

64a Bulla cruciata sanctissimi domini nostri Pape cōtra turchos. Rome, 22 October 1463. [Mainz: Johann Fust and Peter Schoeffer, 1463.] 6 ff. f°.

Ref: H 261; DeR(M) 81; L-H 18.
N.B: Issued by Pius II to arouse interest and support for his crusade against the Turks. This, and its counterpart in German—see no. 65, below—is the first known instance of a caption printed on a preliminary leaf, the forerunner of the modern titlepage. Caption title not present in all copies of the Latin edition. (For reproduction, see LEHMANN-HAUPT, H. *Peter Schoeffer*, 1950, p. 54. See also his notes, no. 12 on p. 63, and no. 14 on p. 84.)

64b —— [*German*]: Dis' ist die bul zu dutsch die vnser allerheiligster vatter der babst Pius herusz gesant hait widder die snoden vngleubigen turcken. [Mainz: Johann Fust and Peter Schoeffer, 1463.] 8 ff.

Ref: H 263; DeR(M) 82; L-H 19.

N.B: This shares with certain copies of the Latin issue, noted above, the honor of having the first label-title.

[65] SENECA. *See* Supplementary Section: *Undated Imprints currently unassigned, or re-assigned to 1470 or later.*

THOMAS Aquinas, *St., c.* 1225–1274.

66 Summa theologicae: Pars secunda, Secunda pars. [Strasbourg: Johann Mentelin, not after 1463.] f°.

Ref: HC *1454; BMC I 51; Stillwell T167; Goff T-208.

N.B: Hain *1454 cites a copy in "bibl. reg. Monacensi" as having the manuscript date 1466; but a copy at Sélestat bears the purchase date of Advent, 1463—*Catalogue générale de la Bibliothèque municipale de Sélestat*, pt. 3, no. 474. No. 130 in MICHELITSCH, A. Thomasschriften, Graz, 1913.

1464

[67] Durand. *See* Supplementary Section: *Undated Imprints currently unassigned, or re-assigned to 1470 or later.*

[68] Nider. *See* Supplementary Section: *Undated Imprints currently unassigned, or re-assigned to 1470 or later.*

RADULPHUS, *Frater.*

69 Indulgentia, 1464 (to benefactors of the Order of the Holy Trinity). [Mainz: Johann Fust and Peter Schoeffer, 1464.] Bdsde. 22 ll.

Ref: HEHCat 5; L-H 20; Stillwell R6; Goff R-4.

1465

ANDREAE, Joannes (Giovanni D'Andrea), *jurist, c.* 1270–1348.

70 Super arboribus consanguinitatis et affinitatis. Glossa in Sextum. (*Issued with* BONIFACIUS VIII. Liber sextus Decretalium. Mainz: Fust and Schoeffer, 17 December, 1465—see no. 71, below.)

BONIFACIUS VIII, *Pont. Max.* (Benedetto Gaetano), *c.* 1235–1303.

71 Liber sextus Decretalium (Comm: Joannes Andreae, *jurist*). Mainz: Johann Fust and Peter Schoeffer, 17 December, 1465. f°.

> *Add*: ANDREAE, Joannes (Giovanni D'Andrea), *jurist, c.* 1270–1348. Super arboribus consanguinitatis et affinitatis.
>
> *Ref*: GW 4848; BMC I 23; DeR(M) 83; L-H 22; Stillwell B869; Goff B-976.
>
> *N.B*: First edition of both works. Variant colophon known. The Bonifacius is a compilation of Canon Law covering the period from 1234 to 1298.

CICERO, Marcus Tullius, 106–43 B.C.

72 De officiis. [Cologne: Ulrich Zel, *c.* 1465.] 4°.

> *Ref*: GW 6914; HC 5233; BMC I 179.
>
> *N.B*: The first separate edition of the *De officiis*. Presumably Zel's first imprint, for although unsigned and undated, it appears from its technique to be earlier than his edition of Joannes Chrysostomus, which is signed and dated 1466. Zel group A, no. 1 (BMC).
>
> *Mon*: VOULLIÉME, E. *Der Buchdruck Kölns bis zum Ende des fünfzehnten Jahrhunderts.* Bonn, 1903 (Gesellschaft für Rheinische Geschichtskunde XXIV.) COSTEN, Severin. *Die Anfänge des Kölner Buchdrucks*, 1957. JUCHHOFF, Rudolf. *Die Universität Köln und die frühen Typographen* (p. 233–243 in *Festschrift für Josef Benzing*, Wiesbaden, 1964).

73 De officiis. Paradoxa Stoicorum. [Mainz:] Johann Fust and Peter Schoeffer, 1465. f°.

> *Add*: HORATIUS FLACCUS, Quintus, 65–8 B.C. Ad T. Manlium Torquatum de vite humane brevitate.
>
> *Ref*: GW 6921; HR 5238; BMC I 23; DeR(M) 84; L-H 6, 21; Stillwell C521; Goff C-575.
>
> *N.B*: The first dated printing of each of the titles included. The text includes seven lines of medieval Latin verse beginning *Tullius Hesperios* ... (see A. Reese. *Anthologia Latina* I i no. 784) and a collection of post-classical verses by various authors (*ibid*, nos. 603–14) entitled *Hexasticha XII sapientum de titulo Ciceronis*. Greek quotations are set in an incomplete Greek font, in which some characters are supplied from the text type. Colophon reads: Presens Marci tulij clarissimū opus. Johannes fust Mogūtinus ciuis. nō atramēto. plumali cāna necq3 aerea. Sed arte quadam perpulcra. Petri manu pueri mei feliciter effeci finitum. Anno.M.cccc.lxv. [For a note on the status of Peter Schoeffer, whom Fust here designates as "puer meus," see no. 87 below.]

74 De oratore. [Subiaco: Konrad Sweynheim and Arnold Pannartz, before 30 September, 1465.] 4°.

> *Ref*: GW 6742; H★5098; BMC IV 1; Pell 3660; Stillwell C593; Goff C-654.
>
> *N.B*: The first edition of the *De oratore* and the first Italian imprint extant. [For a

1465—Cicero (*continued*)

Donatus of apparently earlier date but of which no copy is known, see no. 76, below.] In a copy in the Gewerbemuseum at Leipzig a private owner inscribed the date "Pridie Kal. octobres M.cccc.lxv" [*i.e.*, 30 September, 1465] as the time when he finished annotating his copy.

Mon: SCHOLDERER, Victor. *Printers and readers in Italy in the fifteenth century* (p. 202 ff. in his *Fifty essays*, 1966).

75 Paradoxa Stoicorum. (*Issued with his* De officiis, *etc.* [Mainz:] Johann Fust and Peter Schoeffer, 1465—see no. 73, above.)

DONATUS, Aelius, *fourth century.*

76 Ars minor. [Subiaco: Konrad Sweynheim and Arnold Pannartz, before 30 September, 1465.]

Ref: BMC IV 15.

N.B: The first recorded Italian imprint—*no copy known*. Entered at the head of the printers' list of publications—in a prefatory letter dated 20 March, 1472, addressed to Sixtus IV on behalf of the printers by Joannes Andreae, Bishop of Aleria, editor of their edition of the *Postilla* of Nicolaus de Lyra, Rome, 1471–1472, vol. V (Stillwell N108; Goff N-131)—above an edition of Cicero, *De oratore*, the Leipzig copy of which has the manuscript date 30 September, 1465—*see no. 74, above.* The list of 1472 states that 300 copies were printed of this Donatus and enters it as "inde initium imprimendi sumpsimus." [For the earliest Italian imprint extant, see no. 74, above.]

Mon: SCHOLDERER, Victor. *The Petition of Sweynheim and Pannartz to Sixtus IV* (p. 72–73 in his *Fifty essays*, 1966) relates to the petition but without reference to this item.

HORATIUS FLACCUS, Quintus, 65–8 B.C.

77 Ad T. Manlium Torquatum de vite humane brevitate. (*Issued with* CICERO. De officiis . . . [Mainz:] Johann Fust and Peter Schoeffer, 1465—see no. 73, above.)

LACTANTIUS FIRMIANUS, Caelius (*called* "The Christian Cicero"), *fl.* 260–340.

78 Opera. Subiaco: [Konrad Sweynheim and Arnold Pannartz] 29 October, 1465. f°.

Ref: H *9806; BMC IV 2; Polain 2418; Stillwell L1; Goff L-1.

N.B: The first *extant, dated* book printed in Italy. Preceded by a Donatus (now lost; see no. 76, above) and an undated Cicero (see no. 74, above). In the handsome semi-gothic type employed by the firm during its stay in Subiaco (for reproduction, see WINSHIP, G. P. *Gutenberg to Plantin*, 1926, p. 25). The first complete font of Greek letters was cut for this book; a less complete, small type appeared in a Fust and Schoeffer Cicero issued during the same year (see no. 73, above). In his concept of the universe, Lactantius vigorously denied the roundness of the world.

PONTANO, Ludovico (Ludovicus Pontanus,) *jurist,* 1409–1439.

[79a] Singularia in causis criminalibus. *See* Appendix B: Undated imprints assigned to The Netherlands, no. B: 12.

SALICETO (Guglielmo Saliceto), 1210–1270.

[79b] De salute corporis. *See* Appendix B: Undated imprints assigned to The Netherlands, no. B: 15.

1466

ALPHABETUM divini amoris.

80 —— [Cologne: Ulrich Zel, 1466/67.] 4°.

 Ref: GW 1554; BMC I 179; Stillwell A464; Goff A-524.
 N.B: Attributed in the fifteenth century to Joannes Gerson, and in the sixteenth century to Johann Nider. Gerson's name appears in the colophon of this edition. Zel group A, no. 4 (BMC).

AUGUSTINUS, Aurelius, *St., Bp. of Hippo,* 354–430.

81 De arte praedicandi *(Book IV of* 'De doctrina christiana'). [Strasbourg:] Johann Mentelin [not after 1466]. f°.

 Ref: GW 2871; H* 1956; BMC I 52; Pell 1472; Stillwell A1085; Goff A-1226.
 N.B: The British Museum copy has a rubricator's date, 1466. The printer, Johann Mentelin, is named in the preface. In this first edition, in the AmBM copy and doubtless in others, as characteristic of early technique, the paper was put in position by the registering of holes made by four press-points. In Mentelin's later edition, about 1468 (Goff A-1228), the paper was registered by means of two. An undated edition naming Johann Fust as printer in its preface was issued at Mainz [*see no. 82*].

82 —— [Mainz:] Johann Fust [1466?; before 6 March 1467]. f°.

 Ref: GW 2872; H *1957; BMC I 21; L-H 25; Stillwell A1086; Goff A-1227.
 N.B: This edition and that entered above as no. 81 follow one another so closely it would seem that one was copied from the other. In no. 81 the preface states it was printed by Johann Mentelin; in no. 82 the name of Johann Fust appears in the same position. The preface in both instances states that the book was made

29

1466—Augustinus (continued)

after collating all copies in Heidelberg, Speier, Worms, "and at last also in Strasbourg." This latter phrase, coupled with the fact that certain index-references which were left to be supplied by hand in the Mentelin edition are printed in Fust's edition, suggests that Mentelin's may have been the earlier. For further discussion, see F. W. HOUSEHOLDER (*The Library*, 1943, Series IV, v. 24, nos. 1–2).

A copy of the Mentelin edition at the British Museum has the date "1466" in a contemporary hand. No date is known for Fust's edition, but as Johann Fust died in 1466 [probably in October], it is presumable that it was printed before or issued soon after his death. A terminal date is provided by the fact that Peter Schoeffer, Fust's employee and successor, issued his first book alone [no. 118, below] on 6 March, 1467.

BIBLIA, 45-lines [*Latin*].

83 —— [Strasbourg: Heinrich Eggestein, before 24 May, 1466.] f°.

Ref: GW 4205; H ★3037; BMC I 66; Stillwell B464; Goff B-530.

N.B: The first of three Bibles published by Eggestein during this decade. A copy of this edition at Munich has the rubricator's date, 24 May, 1466.

BIBLIA, 61-lines [*German*].

84 —— [Strasbourg: Johann Mentelin, before 27 June, 1466.] f°.

Ref: GW 4295; HC ★3130; BMC I 52; Pell 2368; Stillwell B558; Goff B-624.

N.B: The first Bible printed in the vernacular although two editions of simplified extracts, the so-called *Biblia Pauperum*, had already been issued in German at Bamberg by Pfister (see nos. 52 and 62). A copy at Stuttgart states in a manuscript colophon that it was printed by Johann Mentelin at Strasbourg, and a copy at Munich has a note of purchase dated 27 June, 1466.

BONAVENTURA, *St., Cardinal,* 1221–1274.

85 Auctoritates utriusque Testamenti. [Strasbourg: Heinrich Eggestein, 1466 or later.] f°.

Ref: BMC I 66; C 1157; Pell 2578; Stillwell B758; Goff B-846.

N.B: According to GW IV, col. 387, an erroneous ascription of a work attributable to Nicolaus de Hanapis. It frequently happened in the fifteenth century and even later that the name of the "Doctor seraphicus" was applied to works written by others. As E. Ph. Goldschmidt once wrote, "It would almost seem as if 'Bonaventura' came . . . to designate a certain type of text, rather than an assertion of authorship." In BMC this edition is placed directly after two undated Bibles (see nos. 83, 84), the first of which (in the Munich copy) has the manuscript date, 24 May, 1466.

BRUNNER, Johann (Joannes Fons), *corrector of the press, fl.* 1445–1468.

86 Grammatica rhythmica. Mainz: Johann [Fust] "Actis terdeni iubilaminis octo bis annis" [1466 or later]. f°.

Cop: Manchester; Paris.
Ref: GW 5591; Pell 5295; L-H 23; DeR(M) 86.
N.B: Although usually assigned to 1466, Dr. Hans Nachod in his paper on *The first book of a living author ever printed* (Kraus, H. P. *Rare Books*, VII, no. 4, May, 1954) presents cause for thinking that it was not printed until after the close of that year. Variously assigned to the press of Peter Schoeffer after the death of Johann Fust. Re-issued in 1468 (no. 130). Authorship questioned.
Mon: SCHOLDERER, V. *Grammatica rhythmica* (p. 52–54 in *Gutenberg Jahrbuch*, 1964). (Reprinted, p. 293–294 in his *Fifty Essays*, Amsterdam, 1966.) [For a note on Brunner, see LEHMANN-HAUPT, H. *Peter Schoeffer*, Rochester, 1950, p. 83.]

CICERO, Marcus Tullius, 106–43 B.C.

87 De officiis. Paradoxa Stoicorum. [Mainz:] Johann Fust and Peter Schoeffer, 4 February, 1466. f°.

Add: HORATIUS FLACCUS, Q., 65–8 B.C. Ad T. Manilium Torquatum. De vite humane brevitate.
Ref: GW 6922; H *5239; BMC I 24; DeR(M) 85; L-H 24; Stillwell C522; Goff C-576.
N.B: Fust's second edition, set in close imitation of that of 1465 (see no. 73, above). The colophon includes the following statement by Johann Fust indicating Schoeffer's status in his printing shop in 1466: *Sed arte quadam perpulcra. manu Petri de gernsshem pueri mei feliciter effeci finitum* . . . For a similar statement by Fust, see no. 73, above.

According to Dr. Aloys Ruppel (as quoted by Dr. Hellmut Lehmann-Haupt in his monograph on *Peter Schoeffer*, Rochester, 1950, p. 6) the term "puer" in medieval usage does not mean either partner or son-in-law, as it has frequently been translated. Instead, it "always designates an employee, working for a salary in a position of dependency upon his employer, regardless of age." Thus it appears that in the year of Fust's death (1466), Peter Schoeffer was still a paid employee, and the various hypotheses assuming that Schoeffer was Fust's partner, adopted son, or son-in-law are without foundation. His name first appears in connection with printing in 1457 (see no. 18, above), although he is known to have been in Mainz in 1455, when he witnessed an oath of veracity on Fust's behalf before a notary in November of that year (*see* Appendix A, 1455).

88 Paradoxa Stoicorum. (*Issued with his* De officiis, *etc.* [Mainz:] Johann Fust and Peter Schoeffer, 4 February, 1466—see no. 87, above.)

1466—(*continued*)

GERSON (Jean Charlier de Gerson; *called* Johannes Gerson), *Chancellor of the University of Paris*, 1363–1429.

> Alphabetum divini amoris. See no. 80, above.

89   Forma absolutionis sacramentalis. (*Issued with his* De pollutione nocturna. [Cologne: Ulrich Zel, 1466/67.]—see no. 90, below.)

90   De pollutione nocturna. Forma absolutionis sacramentalis. [Cologne: Ulrich Zel, 1466/67.] 4°.

> *Ref*: HC ★7694; BMC I 179; Klebs 459.1; Pell 5219; Stillwell G234; Goff G-254.
> *N.B*: Zel group A, no. 3 (BMC).

HORATIUS FLACCUS, Quintus, 65–8 B.C.

91   Ad T. Manlium Torquatum, De vite humane brevitate [Carmen IV 7]. (*Issued with* CICERO, De officiis . . . [Mainz:] Johann Fust and Peter Schoeffer, 4 February, 1466—see no. 87, above.)

JOANNES Chrysostomus, St., *Patriarch of Constantinople* (*sometimes called* The Golden-Tongued), *d.* 407.

92   Homiliae super Matthaeum (Tr: Georgius Trapezuntius, 1396–1486). [Strasbourg: Johann Mentelin, not after 1466.] f°.

> *Ref*: HC ★5034; BMC I 51; Stillwell J255; Goff J-288.
> *N.B*: A copy at the John Rylands Library has the manuscript date 1466. The translator's name appears in the colophon in the phrase "edita a Georio [sic] trapezoncio" and in the dedicatory epistle as "Georgius trapezuntin[9]." But in modern texts, in spite of the fact that he was born in Crete, he is frequently and inaccurately called George of Trepizond—see THORNDIKE, Lynn. *History of magic and experimental science*, IV, p. 697–698.

93   Sermo super psalmum L: *Miserere mei Deus*. [Cologne:] Ulrich Zel, 1466. 4°.

> *Ref*: H 5032; BMC I 179; Polain 2267; Stillwell J264; Goff J-297.
> *N.B*: Zel group A, no. 2 (BMC). Zel's first dated book; preceded by his undated Cicero [1465].

NICOLAUS de Hanapis. *See* BONAVENTURA, St. Auctoriatis utriusque Testamenti. [Strasbourg, *c.* 1466]—no. 85, above.

NIDER, Johann (Hansen Nÿder), 1380–1438. *See* ALPHABETUM divini amoris. [Cologne: Ulrich Zel, 1466/67.]—no. 80, above.

PIUS II, *Pont. Max.* (Eneas Sylvio Piccolomini) 1405–1464.

94   Indulgentia, 1466 (For the benefit of the Church of the Holy Cross at Stuttgart).   [Strasbourg: Johann Mentelin, before 13 April, 1466.] Bdsde. 21 ll.

   Ref: Einbl 63; Cop 88.
   Cop: St. Gallen, *unique* (with inserted date, 13 April).

THOMAS Aquinas, *St.*
   Summa theologicae: Pars secunda, Secunda pars.   (*Transferred to 1463.* See no. 66.)

1467

AUGUSTINUS, Aurelius, *St., Bp. of Hippo*, 354–430.

96   De civitate dei. [Subiaco: Konrad Sweynheim and Arnold Pannartz] 12 June, 1467. f°.

   Ref: GW 2874; H 2046; BMC IV 2; Pell 1545; Stillwell A1089; Goff A-1230.
   N.B: First edition. The last book issued by Sweynheim and Pannartz before their removal to Rome, where, before the year was out, they issued an edition of Cicero's *Epistolae ad familiares*—no. 104 below.

97   De ebrietate. (*Issued with his* Sermo super orationem dominicam. [Cologne: Ulrich Zel, 1467/68.]—*see no. 100, below.*)

98   Enchiridion de fide, spe et caritate. [Cologne: Ulrich Zel, 1467/68.] 4°.

   Ref: GW 2903; HC ★2028; BMC I 181; Stillwell A1124; Goff A-1265.
   N.B: Zel group B, no. 6 (BMC).

99   Expositio super symbolum. (*Issued with his* Sermo super orationem dominicam. [Cologne: Ulrich Zel, 1467/68.]—*see no. 100, below.*)

100   Sermo super orationem dominicam. Expositio super symbolum. De ebrietate. [Cologne: Ulrich Zel, 1467/68.] 4°.

   Ref: GW 2995 (*Pseudo*); HC 1988 = H ★1991; BMC I 181; Pell 1500; Stillwell A1156; Goff A-1302.
   N.B: Zel group B, no. 7 (BMC).

101   De singularitate clericorum. (*Issued with his* De vita christiana. [Cologne:] Ulrich Zel, 1467—*see no. 102, below.*)

102 De vita christiana. De singularitate clericorum. [Cologne:] Ulrich Zel, 1467. 4°.

> *Ref*: GW 3038 (*Pseudo*); HC ★2094 (incl. H ★2082); Pell 1586; Stillwell A1206; Goff A-1355.
> *N.B*: Zel group A, no. 5 (BMC). An early use of leading between lines occurs in the first two leaves of text.

BENEDICTUS XII, *Pont. Max.* (Jacques Fournier), *d.* 1342.

103 *Bulla*: Ad regimen universalis ecclesiae. (*Issued with* CLEMENS V, *Pont. Max.* Constitutiones. Mainz: Peter Schoeffer, 8 October, 1467— *see no. 107a, below.*)

CICERO, Marcus Tullius, 106–43 B.C.

104 Epistolae ad familiares. Rome: Konrad Sweynheim and Arnold Pannartz, in domo Petri de Maximo, 1467. 4°.

> *Ref*: GW 6799; HR 5162; Pr 3290; Pell 3589.
> *N.B*: First edition. Presumably the first Roman imprint, since the Torquemada— no. 119, below—which was printed at the rival press of Ulrich Han in Rome, was not issued until 31 December, 1467. In moving from Subiaco to Rome, Sweynheim and Pannartz replaced their former semi-gothic type with the fine roman type used during the remainder of their career.

105 Paradoxa Stoicorum. [Cologne: Ulrich Zel, *c.* 1467.] 4°.

> *Ref*: GW 7009; BMC I 181; Stillwell C560; Goff C-618.
> *N.B*: Zel group B, no. 9 (BMC). The earliest known separate edition of the *Paradoxa*, which first appeared in 1465 with the Mainz edition of Cicero's *De officiis, etc.*— *no. 73, above*.

106 De senectute sive Cato maior de senectute. [Cologne: Ulrich Zel, *c.* 1467.] 4°.

> *Ref*: GW 6979; H 5306; BMC I 181; Pell 3679.
> *N.B*: First edition. Zel group B, no. 8 (BMC).

CLEMENS V, *Pont. Max.* (Bertrand de Goth, Raimundus Bertrandi del Goth) *c.* 1246–1314.

107a Constitutiones (Comm: Joannes Andreae [Giovanni D'Andrea], *jurist, c.* 1270–1348). *Bulla*: Exivi de paradiso [*Rule of St. Francis*]. Mainz: Peter Schoeffer, 8 October, 1467. f°.

Add: JOANNES XXII, *Pont. Max., d.* 1334. *Bulla*: Constitutio execrabilis. BENE-
DICTUS XII, *Pont. Max., d.* 1342. *Bulla*: Ad regimen universalis ecclesiae.

Ref: GW 7078; HC 5411; BMC I 24; L-H 27; Pell 3836; Stillwell C648; Goff
C-711.

N.B: Second edition. First published in 1460—*no. 32, above.*

107b Exivi de paradiso [Rule of St. Francis]. Mainz: Peter Schoeffer, 8
October, 1467—*see no. 107a, above.*

GERSON (Jean Charlier de Gerson; *called* Johannes Gerson), *Chancellor of the
University of Paris*, 1363–1429.

108a De cognitione castitatis et pollutionibus diurnis. (*Issued with his* De
pollutione nocturna. [Cologne: Ulrich Zel, *c.* 1467.]—*see no. 112,
below.*)

108b Conclusiones de diversis materiis moralibus, sive De regulis manda-
torum. [Cologne: Ulrich Zel, *c.* 1467.] 4°.

Ref: HC 7640; BMC I 180; Pell 5141; Stillwell G185; Goff G-202.
N.B: Zel group B, no. 1 (BMC).

109 De modo vivendi omnium fidelium. (*Issued with his* De passionibus
animae. [Cologne: Ulrich Zel, *c.* 1467]—*see no. 111, below.*)

110 Opus tripartitum: De praeceptis decalogi, De confessione, et De arte
moriendi. [Cologne: Ulrich Zel, *c.* 1467.] 4°.

Ref: HC 7653; BMC I 180; Pell 5189; Stillwell G219; Goff G-238.
N.B: Zel group B, no. 2 (BMC).

111 De passionibus animae. De modo vivendi omnium fidelium. [Cologne:
Ulrich Zel, *c.* 1467.] 4°.

Ref: HC 7678; BMC I 180; Pell 5204; Stillwell G228; Goff G-247.
N.B: Zel group B, no. 3 (BMC).

112 De pollutione nocturna. De cognitione castitatis et pollutionibus
diurnis. [Cologne: Ulrich Zel, *c.* 1467.] 4°.

Add: Forma absolutionis.
Ref: H ★7697, 7690; BMC I 180(I); Klebs 459.2, 460.1; Pell 5212, 5135; Schullian
(ArMed) 209; Stillwell G235, G177; Goff G-255, G-194.
N.B: Zel group B, no. 4 (BMC).

JOANNES XXII, *Pont. Max.*, (Jacques d'Euse), *d.* 1334.

113 *Bulla*: Constitutio execrabilis. (*Issued with* CLEMENS V, *Pont. Max.* Constitutiones. Mainz: Peter Schoeffer, 8 October, 1467.—*see no. 107, above.*)

JOANNES Chrysostomus, *St., Patriarch of Constantinople, d.* 407.

114 Sermones de patientia in Job (Ed & Tr: Lilius Tifernas). [Cologne: Ulrich Zel, *c.* 1467.] 4°.

> *Ref*: HC 5024; BMC I 181; Polain 2263; Stillwell J271; Goff J-304.
> *N.B*: Zel group B, no. 5 (BMC).

RABANUS MAURUS (*called* Hrabanus; Raban), *Abp. of Mainz, c.* 776–856.

115 Opus de universo sive De sermonum proprietate. [Strasbourg: The R-Printer (Adolf Rusch), before 20 July (or June), 1467.] f°.

> *Ref*: HC *13699; BMC I 60; Klebs 524.1; Stillw (AIS) 491; Goff R-1.
> *N.B*: An encyclopaedia of universal knowledge, based largely on the *Etymologiae* of Isidore of Sevilla, *c.* 560–636, but in arrangement and method the forerunner of the *Speculum* of Vincent de Beauvais, *c.* 1200–1264. Possibly the earliest printed book to treat of animals and of medicine [but cf: Appendix B:15, and no. 13, above].
>
> The terminal date derives from a contemporary note in the copy at the Bibliothèque Nationale in Paris. This edition now replaces the "1464"/1467 Durand—no. 67—as the earliest imprint assignable to Rusch, and it is possibly the first book printed in a purely roman type—the type used by Sweynheim and Pannartz in Subiaco having been only partially roman, and their first roman-book printed at Rome having perhaps been issued later in 1467 than this mid-summer imprint above. [For type reproduction, see SCHOLDERER, V. *Adolf Rusch and the earliest roman types* (p. 46 in *The Library*, June 1939). See also MORISON, Stanley. *Early humanistic script and the first roman type* (p. 1–29 in *The Library*, 1943.]

RADULPHUS, *Frater.*

116 Indulgentia, 1467 (For the benefit of the Order of the Holy Trinity). [Cologne: Ulrich Zel, 1467.] Bdsde. 20 ll.

> *Ref*: Einbl 1248, 1249.
> *Cop*: Known in two issues, both at the Landesarchiv at Detmold.

THOMAS AQUINAS, *St., c.* 1225–1274.

117 De articulis fidei et ecclesiae sacramentis. [Cologne: Ulrich Zel, *c.* 1467.] 4°.

Ref: C 559; Pell 1022; Voull(K) 1153; Polain 3739; Stillwell T249 [but deleted in Goff, p. 793].

N.B: Assigned to about 1467 by Polain.

118　Summa theologicae: Pars secunda; Secunda pars. Mainz: Peter Schoeffer, 6 March, 1467. f°.

Ref: H *1459; BMC I 24; L-H 26; Pell 1049 (*var*); Stillwell T188; Goff T-209.

N.B: The first book issued by Peter Schoeffer alone, following the death of his employer, Johann Fust. [First published at Strasbourg about 1466—*no. 95, above.*]

TORQUEMADA (*i.e.,* Juan de Torquemada; Joannes de Turrecremata), *Cardinal,* 1388–1468.

119　Meditationes. Rome: Ulrich Han, 31 December, 1467. 4°.

Ref: H 15722; Sander 7403.

N.B: The earliest illustrated book produced in Italy. According to Hain, it has 34 woodcut illustrations.

Fac: Sander, pl. 747/8.

VOCABULARIUS.

120　Vocabularius ex quo. Eltvil: Heinrich Bechtermüntze *and others,* 4 November, 1467. 4°.

Ref: BMC II 313; DeR(M) 95; Ruppel (1939) 186–189, (1947) 175–177, *fac.*

N.B: An abridged Latin-German dictionary. In a modified version of the type of the Balbi *Catholicon* of 1460. Started by Heinrich Bechtermünze (Bechtermüntze), who died shortly before 1467; completed by his brother Nicolaus and Wigand Spyess on 4 November, 1467.

1468

ACCORSO, Francesco (*called* Accursius), 1182–1260.

121　Glossa ordinaria. (*Issued with* JUSTINIANUS. Institutiones. Mainz: Peter Schoeffer, 24 May, 1468—*see no. 140, below.*)

ANTONINO, *St.* (*called* Antoninus Florentinus), *Bp. of Florence,* 1389–1459.

122　Confessionale: Defecerunt scrutantes scrutiniū ... [Cologne: Ulrich Zel, not after 24 June, 1468.] 4°.

Add: JOANNES Chrysostomus, *St., Patriarch of Constantinople, d.* 407. Sermo de poenitentia.

1468—*Antonino* (*continued*)

> *Ref*: GW 2080; BMC I 181; Stillwell A694; Goff A-786.
>
> *N.B*: A copy at the University Library at Breslau has the purchase-date 1469; a copy owned by Mr. E. H. L. Sexton has a rubricator's date of 24 June, 1468; and a copy offered for sale by W. H. Schab in 1957 bears the rubricator's date of 29 August, 1468. Zel group C:1, no. 1 (BMC).

ARISTEAS, *traditional author assigned to the 3rd century B.C.*

123 Interpretatio septuaginta seniorum. (*Issued with* HIERONYMUS, *St.* Epistolae. [Rome: Sixtus Riessinger, 1468(?), not after 1470]—*see no. 137, below.*)

> *N.B*: It is said to be to this work that we owe the fable of the 72 translators in sealed cells on the Isle of Paros [or at Alexandria], who produced identical versions of the Hebrew scriptures in Greek. The Church Fathers are reputedly responsible for the reduction of the number to seventy. Translated into Latin by Matthias Palmerius of Pisa, 1423–1483. First printed as a separate, at Naples, *c.* 1473— GW 2330.

AUGUSTINUS, Aurelius, *St., Bp. of Hippo*, 354–430.

124 De arte praedicandi (*Book IV of* "De doctrina christiana"). [Strasbourg:] Johann Mentelin [*c.* 1468]. f°.

> *Ref*: GW 2873; H★1955; BMC I 53; Stillwell A1087; Goff A-1228.
>
> *N.B*: The printer is named in the preface. First published by Mentelin in or before 1466—*no. 81, above.*

125 De civitate dei. Rome: Konrad Sweynheim and Arnold Pannartz, In domo Petri de Maximo, 1468. f°.

> *Ref*: GW 2875; HC 2047; BMC IV 5; Pell 1546; Stillwell A1090; Goff A-1231.
>
> *N.B*: First published by Sweynheim and Pannartz at Subiaco in 1467—*no. 96, above.*

126 —— (Comm: Thomas Waleys, *fl.* 1349(?) and Nicolaus Triveth, *fl.* 1268–1334). [Strasbourg: Johann Mentelin, not after 1468.] f°.

> *Ref*: GW 2883; H★2056; BMC I 52; Pell 1554; Stillwell A1098; Goff A-1239.
>
> *N.B*: The first edition of the *De civitate dei* to include commentaries. A copy at the John Rylands Library in Manchester has the contemporary manuscript date 1468. The two commentaries were published together at Toulouse by Heinrich Mayer on 12 October 1488 (Goff W-2) without the text of the original.

BIBLIA.

127 —— 45-lines [*Latin*]. [Strasbourg: Heinrich Eggestein, not after 1468.] f°.

Ref: GW 4206; HC 3036; BMC I 66; Pell 2273; Stillwell B465; Goff B-531.

N.B: The second Latin edition of the Bible from this press, the first having been issued about 1466—*no. 83, above.* Copies at Berlin and Regensburg have the rubricator's date 1468, and others at The Hague and Würzburg have the purchase date 1468.

128 —— 47-line [*Latin*]. [Basel: Berthold Ruppel, *c.* 1468.] f°.

Ref: GW 4207 (+ var.); H ★3045; BMC III 714; Stillwell B466; Goff B-532.

N.B: The first Basel imprint—as established through the typographical studies of Dr. Victor Scholderer and Dr. Kurt Ohly. The date assignment rests on three factors. A journeymen printers' strike occurred in Basel in 1471, indicating that printing must have been practiced there for some time before that date. Technical studies, placing this as the earliest, indicate that a second book, a Nicolaus de Lyra (*no. 142a, below*); and possibly a third, a Gregorius (*no. 195, below*), are also assignable to the pre-strike period—each of them as ponderous and time-consuming in production as the Bible. And typographical analyses made by Dr. Ohly indicate that the Gregorius type was recast on a shorter body soon after the 1471 strike, thus confirming the assignment of the Gregorius to the earlier period. For the text relative to the printers' strike at Basel in 1471, see *Basel Taschenbuch für 1863,* p. 250; STEHLIN, K. *Regesten zur Geschichte des Buchdrucks bis zum Jahre 1500,* no. 4.

Mon: For Dr. Scholderer's paper on these imprints see *The Beginnings of Printing at Basel* (p. 50–54 in *The Library,* 5th Ser. III, no. 1, June 1948; reprinted, p. 192–195 in his *Fifty Essays,* Amsterdam, 1966). See also OHLY, Kurt. *Die Anfänge des Buchdrucks in Basel* (p. 247–260 in *Zentralblatt für Bibliothekswesen,* 1940; and GOFF, F. R. *Variations in Berthold Ruppel's Bible, the first book printed in Switzerland* (scheduled to appear in *Gutenberg Jahrbuch,* 1972, and including a review of the successive steps through which the Bible, as the first of the three earliest books produced at Basel, is assigned to the possible date, *c.* 1468).

BONAVENTURA, *St., Cardinal,* 1221–1274.

129 Meditationes vitae Christi. Augsburg: Günther Zainer, 12 March, [14]68. f°.

Ref: GW 4739 (Pseudo); H ★3557; BMC II 315; Stillwell B800; Goff B-893.

N.B: Zainer's first dated book. In a light gothic type, sold in 1470 to Johann Schussler and replaced by heavier type which in some instances Zainer combined with woodcuts, under the 1471 ruling allowing illustrated books to be printed providing the cuts were made by the wood-engravers of Augsburg—*see AmBCat 85.*

BRUNNER, Johann (Joannes Fons), *corrector of the press, fl.* 1445–1468.

130 Grammatica rhythmica, cum commento. Mainz: [Peter Schoeffer] "terseno in anno terdeni jubilaei" [1468]. 4°.

Ref: GW 5592; BMC I 25; L-H 28; Stillwell B1085; Goff B-1223.

1468—Brunner (*continued*)

N.B: Technical points indicate that the commentary may have been issued separately and possibly at a somewhat later date.

Mon: See under no. 86.

CICERO, Marcus Tullius, 106–43 B.C.

131 De oratore. Rome: Ulrich Han, 5 December, 1468. 4°.

Ref: GW 6743; HC 5099; BMC IV 18; Pell 3664; Stillwell C594; Goff C-655.

N.B: Second edition. First issued by Sweynheim and Pannartz at Subiaco in 1465—*no. 74, above.*

132a —— [Rome: Konrad Sweynheim and Arnold Pannartz, 1468/69.] 4°.

Ref: GW 6744; HC ★5105(I); BMC IV 5(I); Stillwell C595; Goff C-656.

N.B: Third edition as a separate. Also issued in a compilation brought out by this firm, 12 January, 1469—*no. 179, below.*

[132b] COLUMNA, Guido de. *See* Supplementary Section: *Undated Imprints currently unassigned, or re-assigned to 1470 or later.*

DONATUS, Aelius, *fourth century.*

133 Ars minor (*in a variant of the 42-line Bible type*). Mainz: Peter Schoeffer [1468/69 or earlier].

Ref: GW 8718; DeR(M) 43; Oates 29; L-H 217.

Cop: Fragments at Cambridge, Paris, and Trier.

N.B: A 35-line edition. With two-color printed initials in red and blue, from the set first used in the 1457 *Psalter.* The colophon, in a copy at the Bibliothèque Nationale in Paris, reads: Explicit donatus. Arte noua imprimendi. seu caracterizandi. per Petrum de gernssheym. in vrbe Moguntina cū suis capitalibus absq3 calami exaratione effigiatus. Since this was signed by Peter Schoeffer alone, it is presumable that it was printed after the death of his employer, Johann Fust.

Fac: GUTENBERG-GESELLSCHAFT. *Veröffentlichungen* XX., Taf. 30–38, 43, 44.

134 —— (——) [Mainz: Peter Schoeffer, 1468/69 or later.]

Ref: Ruppel 1939, 157–159; 1947, 149 ff; L-H 215, 216, 218.

N.B: Three other unsigned editions in 42-line Bible type—a) 26-lines, known in seven fragments of which four show Schoeffer initials (GW 8698–8704); b) 33-lines, known in fifteen fragments of which three show Schoeffer initials (GW 8705-12; 8714-17); and c) 35-lines, four fragments of which each has a Schoeffer initial in red and blue (GW 8719-8722)—are rated by Dr. Ruppel as later than the signed edition above; assigned to about 1471.

[For discussion of a *Neue Donatfragmente in der Type der 42 zeiligen Bibel in Mainz*, see PRESSER, Helmut (p. 47–62 in *Gutenberg Jahrbuch*, 1954). See also his *Weitere Donatfragmente in Gutenberg-Museum zu Mainz. Ergänzung zu dem 1954 mitgeteilten Verzeichnis* (p. 54–58 in *Gutenberg Jahrbuch*, 1959).]

EGGESTEIN, Heinrich, *printer, fl.* 1468–1483.

135 Vir bone veni & vide . . . (A handbill advertising his 41-line Bible, *c.* 1469, *no. 161 below*). [Strasbourg: Heinrich Eggestein, *c.* 1468.] Bdsde. 22 ll.

Ref: GW 9245; Einbl 529; Ehrman p. 32.
Cop: Munich, *unique*.
Fac: BURGER, C. *Buchhändleranzeigen des XV Jahrhunderts*, 1907, no. 2. LEH-MANN-HAUPT, H. *Peter Schoeffer*, 1950, p. 87. WINSHIP, G. P. *Printing in the fifteenth century*, 1940, p. 45.

HIERONYMUS, *St.*, (St. Jerome), *fl.* 350–420.

136 Epistolae (Ed: Joannes Andreae [Giovanni D'Andrea de' Bossi], *Bp. of Aleria, Papal Librarian, fl.* 1440–1470). Rome: in domo magnifici viri Petri de Maximo [Sweynheim and Pannartz], 13 December, 1468. f°.

Ref: HCR 8551; BMC IV 5; Pr 3294; Stillwell H148; Goff H-161.
N.B: First edition. The *Epistolae* cover fifty years of his life and are addressed to many high-ranking churchmen. The printers are named in a prefatory dedication.

137 —— (Ed: Theodorus Lelius). [Rome: Sixtus Riessinger, 1468(?), not after 1470.]

Add: ARISTEAS., *traditional author assigned to the third century* B.C. Interpretatio septuaginta seniorum (Tr: Matthias Palmierus, 1423–1483).
Ref: HC ★8550; BMC IV p. ix–x, 27; Stillwell H150; Goff H-163.
N.B: A note in the Chantilly copy written by Johannes Hynderbach, Bishop of Trent, has the manuscript date 1470 (BMC). If not completed by 1468 as variously believed, it would seem that this massive work must at least have been on the press by that date.

INNOCENTIUS III, *Pont. Max.* (Lothario de' Conti; Lotharius), *d.* 1216.

138 De miseria humane condicionis sive Liber de contemptu mundi. [Germany: Eponymous press, printer of Lotharius, 1468? or later.] f°.

Ref: H ★10209; BMC III 707; Stillwell 177; Goff I-84.
N.B: On the recto of the first page of text, as noted in Hain, there appears the printed date M.cccc.xlviij, which has been the subject of various interpretations.

1468—(continued)

JOANNES Chrysostomus, *St., Patriarch of Constantinople (sometimes called* Chrysostomus, *i.e., the Golden-Tongued), d. 407.*

139a Sermo de poenitentia. (*Issued with* Antonino, *St.* Confessionale . . . [Cologne: Ulrich Zel, not after 24 June, 1468.]—*see no. 122, above.*)

139b Sermo super psalmum L: *Miserere mei Deus.* [Cologne: Ulrich Zel, 1468 or earlier.] 4°.

> *Ref:* HC★5031; Pr 809; Polain 2266; Stillwell J265; Goff J-298.
> *N.B:* The assignment, *c.* 1468, derives from Polain.

JUSTINIANUS, Flavius Anicius, *Emperor of the Eastern Roman Empire*, 483–565.

140 Institutiones (with the *Glossa ordinaria* of Accorso, 1182–1260). Mainz: Peter Schoeffer, 24 May, 1468. f°.

> *Ref:* GW 7580; H★9489; BMC I 25; L-H 29; Stillwell J456; Goff J-506.
> *N.B:* The first edition of any of the four codices of Roman law known as the *Corpus Juris Civilis* of Justinian. Contains the first printed eulogy to the invention of printing and marks the beginning of Schoeffer's advertising campaign, a few months after Gutenberg's death (see Appendix A: 1468). [It is interesting to note that a proof-sheet from one of Schoeffer's editions of Justinian (L-H, plate 9) shows in its margin various correctional symbols similar to those used in proof-reading today.]
> *Fac:* LEHMANN-HAUPT, H. *Peter Schoeffer*, 1950, plate 8.

LACTANTIUS FIRMIANUS, Caelius (*called* "The Christian Cicero"), *fl.* 260–340.

141 Opera. Rome: Konrad Sweynheim and Arnold Pannartz, in domo Petri de Maximo, 1468. f°.

> *Ref:* H★9807; BMC IV 4; Pr 3291; Stillwell L2; Goff L-2.
> *N.B:* Second edition, without the Greek characters which appeared in the Subiaco edition of 1465—*no. 78, above.*

NICOLAUS de Lyra (Nicolas de Lyre), *O.M., c.* 1270–1349.

142a Postilla super quattuor Evangelistas. [Basel: Berthold Ruppel, 1468/69.] f°.

> *Ref:* HC★10384; BMC III 714; Polain 2827; Stillwell N105; Goff N-128.
> *N.B:* According to the Scholderer and Ohly analyses, this now ranks as the second of three books presumably printed at Basel before the printers' strike of 1471. (For discussion, *see no. 128, above.*)

NIDER, Johann, 1380–1438.

142b De contractibus mercatorum. [Cologne: Ulrich Zel, 1468/70.] 4°.

> *Add*: Johannes de Nigro Monte. Articuli contra impugnantes privilegia ordinis praedicatorum.
>
> *Ref*: HC ★11822; BMC I 185; Polain 2887; Voull(K) 863; Oates 328; Stillwell N149; Goff N-170.
>
> *N.B*: Discusses the payment of interest (SMITH, David E. *History of mathematics*, New York, 1923–25. II, p. 563). Zel group C:2 (BMC).

PETRUS LOMBARDUS, Bp. of Paris, *d.* 1160.

143 Sententiarum Libri IV. [Strasbourg: Printer of "Henricus Arminensis" (Georg Reyser), not after 1468.] f°.

> *Ref*: H ★10184; BMC I 76; Stillwell P434; Goff P-478.
>
> *N.B*: First edition of the work upon which generations of scholars had sharpened their scholastic wits. A copy at the University of Toronto has a rubricator's date 1468.
>
> *Mon*: OHLY, Kurt. *Georg Reysers Wirken in Strassburg und Würzburg. Zum Problem des Druckers des Henricus Ariminensis* (p. 121–140 in *Gutenberg Jahrbuch*, 1956.)

PHALARIS, *traditional author, sixth century B.C.*

144 Epistolae (Tr: Franciscus Aretinus). [Rome: Ulrich Han, 1468/69.] f°.

> *Ref*: BMC IV 19; Pr 3340; Stillwell P500; Goff P-546.
>
> *N.B*: Imaginary letters composed seven hundred years or more after Phalaris's death. First edition. Although accepted as authentic for many centuries, Phalaris's authorship of the *Epistolae* was disproved through the analysis of Richard Bentley, published in 1699. [For a summary of Bentley's arguments, see HIGHET, G. *The classical tradition*, 1950, p. 283–284.] The Goff Census lists twenty editions in Latin before 1499; five in Italian, 1471–1489; and one in Greek, 18 June, 1498.

RODERICUS Zamorensis (*called* Sánchez de Arévalo, Rodrigo), *Bp. of Oviedo and Zamora*, 1404–1470.

145 Speculum vitae humanae. Rome: Konrad Sweynheim and Arnold Pannartz, 1468. 4°.

> *Ref*: HC ★13939; BMC IV 4; Stillwell R208; Goff R-214.
>
> *N.B*: First edition.
>
> *Fac*: GOFF, F. R. *The earliest instance of printing on vellum in an Italian book* (p. 80–85 in *Gutenberg Jahrbuch*, 1966).

1468—(continued)

THOMAS Aquinas, *St.*, *c.* 1225–1274.

146 Summa theologicae, pars prima.   [Cologne: Ulrich Zel, 1468 or earlier.] f°.

> *Ref*: H 1439; BMC I 191; Pr 879.
> *N.B*: The first edition of this section of St. Thomas' work on systematic theology. Assigned to about 1468 because the four pinholes in the leaves of the book indicate Zel's earliest method of securing his paper. Since this is a folio, however, it does not appear in BMC's quarto groups of the Zel analysis.

TRIVETH, Nicolaus (Nicholas Trevet), *fl.* 1268–1334, *commentator.*

147 Interpretatio. (*In* AUGUSTINUS, Aurelius, *St.* De civitate dei. [Strasbourg: Johann Mentelin, not after 1468.]—*see no. 126, above.*)

WALEYS, Thomas (Thomas Valois), *fl.* 1349(?), *commentator.*

148 Interpretatio. (*In* AUGUSTINUS, Aurelius, *St.* De civitate dei. [Strasbourg: Johann Mentelin, not after 1468.]—*see no. 126, above.*)

1469

ALBINUS PLATONICUS (*erroneously cited as* Alcinous—GW 806], *fl. second century.*

149 Epitoma disciplinarum Platonis (Tr: Pietro Balbi].   (*Issued with* APULEIUS Madaurensis. Opera. Rome: [Konrad Sweynheim and Arnold Pannartz] 28 Feb. 1469—*see no. 150, below.*]

APULEIUS Madaurensis, Lucius, *fl.* 125.

150 Opera (Metamorphoses, sive De asino aureo . . . With Preface by Joannes Andreae [Giovanni D'Andrea de' Bossi], *Bp. of Aleria, Papal Librarian, fl.* 1440–1470). Rome: in domo Petri de Maximo [Konrad Sweynheim and Arnold Pannartz], 28 February, 1469. f°.

> *Add*: HERMES TRISMEGISTOS, *mythical author ascribed to antiquity.* Asclepius (Tr: Apuleius Madaurensis, *fl.* 125). ALBINUS Platonicus, *second century* [*erroneously cited as Alcinous*—GW 806]. Epitoma disciplinarum Platonis (Tr: Pietro Balbi, *Bp. of Tropea*).
> *Ref*: GW 2301; HC *1314; BMC IV 6; Pell 923; Stillwell A833; Goff A-934.

ARISTOTELES, 384–322 B.C.

151   Ethica ad Nicomachum (Tr: Leonardo Bruni, of Arezzo [Leonardus Brunus Aretinus], 1369–1444). [Strasbourg: Johann Mentelin, before 10 April, 1469.] f°.

> *Add*: Politica. Oeconomica.
> *Ref*: GW 2367; H *1762; BMC I 53; Pell 1238; Stillwell A880; Goff A-983.
> *N.B*: The first edition of Aristotle. A copy at Freiburg im Breisgau has the manuscript date 1469. The copy noted in Burger's *Index*, p. 498, the source of the citation of the purchase date 10 April, 1469, is located at Cambridge University (Oates 87). According to the text, the translation was completed 28 December, 1438.

152   Oeconomica. (*Issued with his* Ethica ad Nicomachum. [Strasbourg: Johann Mentelin, before 10 April, 1469.]—*see no. 151, above*.)

153   Politica. (*Issued with his* Ethica ad Nicomachum. [Strasbourg: Johann Mentelin, before 10 April, 1469.]—*see no. 151, above*.)

ASTESANUS DE AST, O.F.M., *fl.* 1316.

154   Summa de casibus conscientiae. [Strasbourg: Johann Mentelin, not after 1469.] f°.

> *Ref*: GW 2749; H *1888; BMC I 53; Pell 1401; Stillwell A1027; Goff A-1160.
> *N.B*: Two copies provide clues to the date of issue, a purchase-date of 1469 in a copy at Munich and a binder's date in a copy at the Bibliothèque Nationale at Paris.

155   Volentes emere summā . . . [An advertisement of one of Mentelin's editions of the *Summa de casibus conscientiae*]. [Strasbourg: Johann Mentelin, 1469?] Bdsde. 42 ll.

> *Ref*: Einbl 998; Burger (Buch) 7.
> *N.B*: According to BMC I 54, "it seems reasonable to suppose that this elaborate advertisement relates to the first edition [*no. 154, above*] rather than to either of its successors." Einbl 999 describes a similar broadside of 41 lines, at Munich [Burger (Buch) 8]. See also EHRMAN, A. and POLLARD, G. *The distribution of books by catalogue*, Cambridge, 1965, p. 32, no. 6.
> *Fac*: Burger (Buch) 7.

AURBACH, Johannes de (Koppischt, Johann, *von Aurbach, Vicar of the Cathedral School at Bamberg, fl.* 1440–1460.

156   Summa de auditione confessione et de sacramentis. Augsburg: Günther Zainer, 1469. f°.

1469—Aurbach (continued)

> *Ref*: GW 2852; H*2124; BMC II 315; AmBCat 86; Stillwell A1229; Goff A-1381.
>
> *N.B*: The author is not to be confused with Johannes de Auerbach [Johannes Urbach], a jurist and teacher at the University of Erfurt, *fl.* 1405.

BALBI, Giovanni (Johannes Balbus), *d.* 1298.

157 Catholicon. Augsburg: Günther Zainer, 30 April, 1469. f°.

> *Ref*: GW 3183; H*2255; BMC II 315; Pell 1703; Stillwell B20; Goff B-21.
>
> *N.B*: Second edition. According to the text this treatise on the Latin language was completed on 7 March, 1286. For the first edition, brought out at Mainz in 1460, *see no. 30, above.*

BEICHTBUECHLEIN [*German*].

158 *Text begins*: In dem namen der heyligen driualtikeit Amē. [E]s sint vil menschen ... (A manual for confession). [Mainz: Peter Schoeffer, *c.* 1469.] 4°. 14 ff.

> *Ref*: GW 3769; L-H 203; Nachträge 42.
>
> *N.B*: Known only in a unique copy at Aschaffenburg.

BERNARDUS SILVESTER, 1090–1153.

159 Epistola de gubernatione rei familiaris. Augsburg: Günther Zainer, [1469/70]. Bdsde. 60 ll.

> *Ref*: GW 3961 (*Pseudo*); Einbl 441; H*3004.
>
> *Cop*: Leipzig; Munich.
>
> *N.B*: *Text begins*: Incipit epistola Beati bernardi. ad Raymundū nepotem suum ... [Also assigned to Bernard (*d.* 1126), the first great master of the Cathedral School of Chartres. For discussion regarding identity, *see* Thorndike, L. *A history of magic and experimental science.* II. 1923, p. 99 ff.]

BESSARION, *Cardinal, Patriarch of Constantinople, Greek humanist*, 1395–1472.

160 Adversus Platonis calumniatorem. Rome: Konrad Sweynheim and Arnold Pannartz [before 13 September, 1469]. f°.

> *Ref*: GW 4183; HC 3004; BMC IV 7; Pell 2253; Stillwell B453; Goff B-518.
>
> *N.B*: According to Audiffredi, Bessarion mentions this work as "nuper editum" in a letter to Marsilio Ficino, 13 September, 1469. The colophon contains the following statement regarding the whereabouts of the firm's printing-house, "Petrus cum fratre Francisco Maximus ambo Huic operi aptatam contribuere domum." Written in controversy with Georgius Trapezuntius of Crete (the so-called George of Trepizond), 1396–*c.*1451—*see* THORNDIKE, Lynn. *History of magic and experimental science.* IV, 697–698.

BIBLIA, 41-lines [*Latin*].

161 —— [Strasbourg: Heinrich Eggestein, *c.* 1469]. f°.

> *Ref*: GW 4208; H ★3035; BMC I 66; Pell 2267; Stillwell B467; Goff B-533.
> *N.B*: Somewhat later than two other Eggestein editions of the Latin Bible (*see nos. 83, 127*), which have rubricators' dates of 1466 and 1468. For handbill advertising this work, *see no. 135.*

BIBLIA, 60-line [*German*].

162 —— [Strasbourg: Heinrich Eggestein, 1469/70.] f°.

> *Ref*: GW 4296; HC ★3129; BMC I 72; Pell 2369; Stillwell B559; Goff B-625.
> *N.B*: A copy at Gotha has an ownership date of 1470. (The Bible was first published in German by Johann Mentelin, *c.* 1466—*no. 84, above*).

CAESAR, Caius Julius, *c.* 100–44 B.C.

163 Commentarii (Ed: Joannes Andreae [Giovanni D'Andrea de' Bossi], *Bp. of Aleria, Papal Librarian, fl.* 1440–1470). Rome: In Domo Petri de Maximis [Konrad Sweynheim and Arnold Pannartz], 12 May, 1469. f°.

> *Ref*: GW 5863; HC ★4212; BMC IV 7; Pell 3139; Stillwell C13; Goff C-16.
> *N.B*: First edition. Contains Bellum Gallicum, Bellum civile, Bellum Alexandrinus, Africum, Hispaniense. Issued in an edition of 275 copies. With a table of rubrics on leaf 167 *verso*.

CICERO, Marcus Tullius, 106–43 B.C.

164 De amicitia, sive Laelius de amicitia. [Rome: Ulrich Han, *c.* 1469.] f°.

> *Ref*: GW 6993; BMC IV 19(?).
> *N.B*: The first separate edition of *De amicitia*.

165 —— (*Issued with his* De officiis, *etc.* Rome: [Sweynheim and Pannartz], 24 January, 1469—*see no. 175, below*.)

166 —— (*Issued with his* De officiis, *etc.* [Rome: Ulrich Han, *c.* 1469]—*see no. 174, below*.)

167 —— (*Issued with his* De officiis, *etc.* [Rome: Ulrich Han, *c.* 1469/70]—*see no. 176, below*.)

168 Brutus. Orator. Rome: in domo magnifici viri Petri de Maximo [Konrad Sweynheim and Arnold Pannartz], 12 January, 1469. 4°.

1469—Cicero (*continued*)

> *Ref*: GW 6754; HC 5105:2; BMC IV 5 (II); Stillwell C582; Goff C-643.
> *N.B*: Presumably the first edition of each of these works.

169 —— (*Issued with his* De oratore. Rome: In domo Petri de Maximo [Konrad Sweynheim and Arnold Pannartz], 12 January, 1469—*see no. 179, below.*)

170 Epistolae ad familiares. [Venice:] Johann von Speier, [before 18 September] 1469. f°.

> *Ref*: GW 6800; HC 5164; BMC V 152; Stillwell C454; Goff C-504.
> *N.B*: The first of two 1469 editions from this Venetian press. Issued in only a hundred copies, possibly to test the market. The date is derived from the official privilege, granted 18 September, 1469, in which this is mentioned as already issued.

171 —— Venice: Johann von Speier, 1469. f°.

> *Ref*: GW 6801; HC 5165; BMC V 153; Stillwell C455; Goff C-505.
> *N.B*: The second of two 1469 editions from this Venetian press. The colophon states that it was issued in three hundred copies, four months after the earlier edition.

172 —— (Ed: Joannes Andreae [Giovanni D'Andrea de' Bossi], *Bp. of Aleria, Papal Librarian, fl.* 1440–1470.) Rome: Konrad Sweynheim and Arnold Pannartz, [after 4 November] 1469. f°.

> *Ref*: GW 6802; HCR 5163; BMC IV 8.
> *N.B*: According to the colophon of this edition, Joannes Andreae completed his revision of the text, or authenticated it, 4 November, 1469.

173 De officiis. [Rome: Ulrich Han, *c.* 1469.] 4°.

> *Ref*: GW 6915.
> *N.B*: The second edition of the *De officiis* as a separate. First issued by Ulrich Zel at Cologne, *c.* 1465—*no. 72, above.*

174 —— [Rome: Ulrich Han, *c.* 1469.] 4°.

> *Add*: Paradoxa Stoicorum. Laelius de amicitia. Cato maior de senectute.
> *Ref*: H 5251; BMC IV 19; Pr 3339; Pell 3721.
> *N.B*: Each title was apparently issued separately and the remainders later brought together in this compilation.

175 —— Rome: In domo magnifici viri Petri de Maximo [Konrad Sweynheim and Arnold Pannartz], 24 January, 1469. 4°.

> *Add*: Paradoxa Stoicorum. Laelius de amicitia. Cato maior de senectute.

Ref: GW 6924; HC 5243; BMC IV 6; Pell 3727.

N.B: The first dated editions of *De amicitia* and of *De senectute*. Included with the text is *Hexasticha xii sapientum de titulo Ciceronis*.

176 —— [Rome: Ulrich Han, *c.* 1469/70.] 4°.

Add: Paradoxa Stoicorum. De amicitia. De senectute. Somnium Scipionis.

Ref: H★5251; BMC IV 19; Pell 3721; Pr 3339.

N.B: Each title was apparently issued separately, and the remainders later issued as a compilation. The *Gesamtkatalog* enters the first three titles as separates (GW 6915, 7010, 6993), but the last two together (GW 6980).

177 Orator, sive De optimo genere dicendi. (*Issued with his* Brutus, *etc.* Rome: [Sweynheim and Pannartz], 12 January, 1469—*no. 168, above*.)

178 —— (*Issued with his* De oratore, *etc.* Rome: [Sweynheim and Pannartz], 12 January, 1469—*no. 179, below*.)

179 De oratore. Brutus, sive De claris oratoribus. Orator, sive De optimo genere dicendi. Rome: In domo magnifici viri Petri de Maximo [Konrad Sweynheim and Arnold Pannartz], 12 January, 1469 [or later?]. 4°.

Ref: GW 6744, 6754; HC 5105; BMC IV 5; Pr 3295; Pell 3665.

N.B: In addition to their being issued in this compilation, the *De oratore* was brought out by this firm in an undated separate, 1468/69—*no. 132, above*, and the *Brutus* and *Orator* were issued together on 12 January, 1469—*no. 168, above*. If the theory is correct that the separates were issued first and that remainders in stock were subsequently combined and re-issued, the date of the compilation would seem to be somewhat later than that appearing on the final page.

180 Paradoxa Stoicorum. [Rome: Ulrich Han, *c.* 1469.] f°.

Ref: GW 7010.

N.B: The second edition of the *Paradoxa* as a separate. For the first separate, *see no. 105, above*. (It had appeared still earlier in a compilation—*no. 73, above*.)

181 —— (*Issued with his* De officiis, *etc.* Rome: [Konrad Sweynheim and Arnold Pannartz], 24 January, 1469—*no. 175, above*.)

182 —— (*Issued with his* De officiis, *etc.* [Rome: Ulrich Han, *c.* 1469]—*no. 174, above*.)

183 —— (*Issued with his* De officiis, *etc.* [Rome: Ulrich Han, *c.* 1469/70]—*no. 176, above*.)

184   De senectute, sive Cato maior de senectute.   [Rome: Ulrich Han,
      c. 1469.]   f°.

> *Add*: Somnium Scipionis.
> *Ref*: GW 6980.
> *N.B*: *De senectute* was first published at Cologne, *c.* 1467—*no. 106, above.*

185   —— (*Issued with his* De officiis, *etc.* Rome: [Konrad Sweynheim and
      Arnold Pannartz, 24 January,] 1469—*no. 175, above.*)

186   —— (*Issued with his* De officiis, *etc.* [Rome: Ulrich Han, *c.* 1469.]—
      no. 174, above.)

187   —— (*Issued with his* De officiis, *etc.* [Rome: Ulrich Han, *c.* 1469/70.]—
      no. 176, above.)

188   Somnium Scipionis. (*Issued with his* De senectute. [Rome: Ulrich Han,
      c. 1469.]—*no. 184, above.*)

189   —— (*Issued with his* De officiis, *etc.* [Rome: Ulrich Han, 1469/70.]—
      no. 176, above.)

190   Tusculanae disputationes.   Rome: Ulrich Han, 1 April, 1469.   f°.

> *Ref*: GW 6888; BMC IV 19; HR 5312; Pell 3777; Stillwell C570; Goff C-630.
> *N.B*: First edition.

DIURNALE Moguntinum.

191   —— [Mainz: Peter Schoeffer, *c.* 1469 ?]

> *Ref*: Pell 4374; DeR(M) 89.
> *N.B*: Known only through two leaves on vellum, at the Bibliothèque Nationale in
> Paris. GW VII col. 530 considers this to be part of a Psalter.

EXPOSITIO super Canonem Missae.

192   —— [Augsburg: Günther Zainer, 1469.]   f°.

> *Ref*: GW 5983; H *6795; BMC II 315; Pell 4693; Stillwell E110; Goff E-140.
> *N.B*: Listed in BMC between two dated entries of 1469.

GELLIUS, Aulus, *fl.* 130–165.

193   Noctes Atticae [*Latin and Greek*]   (Ed: Joannes Andreae [Giovanni
      D'Andrea de' Bossi], *Bp. of Aleria, Papal Librarian, fl.* 1440–1470).

[Rome:] In domo Petri de Maximis [Konrad Sweynheim and Arnold Pannartz], 11 April, 1469. f°.

> *Ref*: HCR 7517; BMC IV 6; Pell 5008; Stillwell G107; Goff G-118.
>
> *N.B*: A compilation of excerpts from ancient writers, many of whose works are otherwise lost.

GERSON (Jean Charlier de Gerson; *called* Johannes Gerson), *Chancellor of the University of Paris*, 1363–1429.

194　De custodia linguae. [Mainz: Peter Schoeffer, 1469/70 (*i.e.* between 13 June, 1469 and 7 September, 1470).] 4°.

> *Ref*: H 7684; BMC I 26; Pell 5164; L-H 34; Stillwell G201; not in Goff.
>
> *N.B*: The terminal-dates derive from the facts that on Schoeffer's 1469/70 advertising-list this title is entered after a Thomas Aquinas of 13 June, 1469, the latest work listed with actual date; and that Schoeffer's edition of Hieronymus, dated 7 September, 1470, must have been printed at some time after the issuing of the list— since it is not entered and, in fact, has a handbill of its own, announcing its publication. The undated titles following the St. Thomas entry would therefore seem to have been issued between the two known dates.

GREGORIUS I, *Pont. Max., St., the Great, c.* 540–604.

195　Moralia sive Exposito in Job. [Basel: Berthold Ruppel, 1469/70.] f°.

> *Ref*: H★7926; BMC III 714; Pell 5376; Stillwell G386; Goff G-426.
>
> *N.B*: Because of a purchase-date of 1468 in the copy at the Bibliothèque Nationale in Paris, the Gregorius was at one time accepted as the first Basel imprint. The purchase-date, however, was shown by Dr. Ernst Schulz to be a forgery, as also the manuscript date "1470" in a copy at the British Museum. The typographical analyses of Dr. Kurt Ohly, as recorded by Dr. Scholderer in his essay on *The Beginning of printing at Basel* (p. 192–195 in his *Fifty essays*, 1966), have placed the Gregorius as the third of the three earliest products from Ruppel's press at Basel (*see nos. 128 and 142, above*), all of them quite certainly issued some time before the Basel printers' strike of 1471.

HERMES TRISMEGISTOS, *mythical author ascribed to antiquity*.

196　Asclepius (Tr: Apuleius Madaurensis). (*Issued with* Apuleius Madaurensis, Lucius, *fl*. 125. Opera. Rome: [Sweynheim and Pannartz] 28 February, 1469—*no. 150, above*.)

HIERONYMUS, *St*. (Saint Jerome), *fl*. 350–420.

197　Epistolae. [Strasbourg: Johann Mentelin, not after 1469.] f°.

> *Ref*: HC★8549; BMC I 53; Stillwell H149; Goff H-162.

1469—Heironymus (continued)
> N.B: The copy at the Bibliothèque Nationale in Paris was bound by Johann Richen-
> bach of Geislingen, in 1469. First published at Rome in 1468—*no. 136, above.*

JOANNES Chrysostomus, *St., Patriarch of Constantinople (sometimes called* Chrysostomus, *i.e.,* The Golden-Tongued), *d.* 407.

198 De eo quod nemo laeditur ab alio nisi a semetipso fuerit laesus. [Cologne: Ulrich Zel, *c.* 1469.] 4°.

> *Ref:* HC 5052; BMC I 182; Stillwell J258; Goff J-291.
> *N.B:* Zel group C:1, no. 3 (BMC).

199 De reparatione lapsi. [Cologne: Ulrich Zel, *c.* 1469.] 4°.

> *Ref:* HC 5051; BMC I 182; Stillwell J261; Goff J-294.
> *N.B:* Zel group C:1, no. 2 (BMC).

200 Sermo de poenitentia. (*Issued with* ANTONINO, *St.* Confessionale: *Defecerunt* . . . [Cologne: Ulrich Zel, "not after 1469"—*i.e.,* not after 24 June, 1468]—*see no. 122, above.*)

JUSTINUS, Marcus Junianus, *fl. third century*(?).

201 Epitome in Trogi Pompeii historias. [Rome:] Ulrich Han [*c.* 1469]. 4°.

> *Ref:* H 9646; BMC IV 19; Stillwell J553; Goff J-614.
> *N.B:* A collection of historical writings by Trogus Pompeius, 59 B.C.–A.D. 17, which are lost except for this abridgement by Justinus and a few excerpts in Pliny. Variations in type measurements in this edition account for the early date assignment, although the type was in use during 1470 and 1471 (*cf.* BMC).

LIVIUS, Titus, 59 B.C.–A.D. 17.

202 Historiae Romanae decades (Ed: Joannes Andreae [Giovanni d'Andrea de' Bossi], *Bp. of Aleria, Papal Librarian, fl.* 1440–1470). Rome: Konrad Sweynheim and Arnold Pannartz [1469]. f°.

> *Ref:* H *10128; BMC IV 8; Stillwell L208; Goff L-236.
> *N.B:* No. 15 in the Sweynheim and Pannartz list of 1472, preceding the entry of the Lucanos of 1469.

203 —— (Ed: Giovanni Antonio Campano, *Bp. of Teramo, c.* 1429–1477. [Rome:] Ulrich Han [1469, before 3 August, 1470]. f°.

> *Ref:* HC 10129; BMC IV 20; Stillwell L209; Goff L-237.

N.B: Mentioned in Campano's preface to the Quintilian of 3 August, 1470. Variations in type measurements account for the early assignment to 1469, although the type was in use during 1470 (*see BMC*).

LUCANUS, Marcus Annaeus, A.D. 39–65.

204 Pharsalia. Lucani vita. (Ed: Joannes Andreae [Giovanni d'Andrea de' Bossi], *Bp. of Aleria, Papal Librarian, fl.* 1440–1470.) Rome: Konrad Sweynheim and Arnold Pannartz, 1469. f°.

> *Ref:* H *10231; BMC IV 9; Stillwell L259; Goff L-292.
> *N.B:* No. 17 on the Sweynheim and Pannartz list of 1472. Issued in an edition of 275 copies.

MENTELIN, Johann, *publisher. See nos.* 155, 205n.

PABLO de SANTA MARIA (Paulus de Sancta Maria; *formerly* Solomon Levi), *Abp. of Burgos, c.* 1350–1435.

205 Scrutinium scripturarum. [Strasbourg: Johann Mentelin, 1469/70.] f°.

> *Ref:* H *10763; BMC I 54; Stillwell P172; Goff P-201.
> *N.B:* Written by a converted Rabbi. For a note on Mentelin's advertisement of this work, see SCHOLDERER, V. *Two unrecorded early book-advertisements* (p. 114–115 in *The Library*, 5th Ser., XI, 1956). See also EHRMAN, A. and G. POLLARD. *The distribution of books by catalogue*, Cambridge, 1965, plate 15. A copy at the John Carter Brown Library has a Richenbach binding dated 1470.

PIUS II, *Pont. Max.* (Eneas Silvio Piccolomini), 1405–1464.

206 De duobus amantibus—Eurialo et Lucretia. [Cologne: Ulrich Zel, *c.* 1469.] 4°.

> *Ref:* H 214; BMC I 182; Voull (K) 943; Polain 3155.
> *N.B:* Zel group C:1, no. 4 (BMC). The early writings of Eneas Silvio Piccolomini, among which this belongs, were retracted when he was elevated to the Papacy, but remained highly popular and were frequently printed.

207 Epistola ad Mahumetem. [Cologne: Ulrich Zel, *c.* 1469.] 4°.

> *Ref:* HC *171; BMC I 182; Stillwell P629; Goff P-696.
> *N.B:* An effort on the part of Pius II to protect Christendom against the Turks. Zel group C:1, no. 5 (BMC).

PLINIUS SECUNDUS, Gaius (Pliny, *the Elder*), A.D. 23–79.

208 Historia naturalis. Venice: Johann von Speier, [before 18 September] 1469. f°.

> *Ref*: HCR 13087; BMC V 153; Klebs 786.1; Stillw (AIS) 487; Goff P-786.
>
> *N.B*: First edition. A scientific encylopaedia in thirty-seven books treating of medi-
> cine, chemistry, botany, geology, mineralogy, husbandry, zoology, the history
> of art, *etc.*, as known in Pliny's time. The terminal-date derives from the fact
> that a Cicero and this Pliny are mentioned as already published, in the five-year
> privilege granted Johann von Speier on 18 September, 1469, by the Signoria of
> Venice.

SCHOEFFER, Peter, *of Gernsheim, publisher, c.* 1430–1503.

209 Volentes sibi comparare infrascriptos libros . . . in huiusmodi littera
moguntie impressos . . . [Handbill advertising the books in his stock.]
Mainz: [Peter Schoeffer, 1469/70, before 7 September, 1470]. Bdsde.
30 ll.

> *Ref*: Einbl 1296; L-H 251; Ehrman 2.
>
> *Cop*: Munich, *unique*.
>
> *N.B*: A single-leaf advertisement of twenty-one books. The first type-specimen sheet
> known. Beneath the list of titles is a line in the handsome *Psalter* type, reading:
> hec est littera psalterij. At the bottom of the handbill is the address in manu-
> script [at the inn "Zum wilden Mann," presumably at Nuremberg] of one of
> Schoeffer's travelling book-agents. In view of the facts that a Hieronymus
> published by Schoeffer on 7 September, 1470 [for which a separate advertise-
> ment was issued] is not mentioned, and that the latest date quoted is that of the
> *Super quarto libro Sententiarum* of Thomas Aquinas of 13 June, 1469, it is pre-
> sumable that the list was printed at some time between the two dates. [For
> Schoeffer's initial venture in advertising, see: Appendix A:2, 1468.]
>
> *Mon*: VELKE, W. *Zu den Bücheranzeigen Peter Schöffers* (GUTENBERG-GESELL-
> SCHAFT. *Veröffentlichungen*, V–VIII, 1908, *facs.*)
>
> *Fac*: MEYER, Wilhelm. *Bücheranzeigen des 15. Jahrhunderts*, Leipzig, 1885 [*Separa-*
> *tabdruck aus dem Centralblatt für Bibliothekswesen*]. LEHMANN-HAUPT, L.
> *Peter Schoeffer*, Rochester, 1950, plate 19. BURGER, K. *Buchändleranzeigen des*
> *15 Jahrhunderts*, Leipzig, 1907, pl. 2.

SERVIUS (Servius Maurus, Honoratus), *grammarian, fl. end of fourth century.*

210 Commentarii in Vergilii opera. [Rome:] Ulrich Han [1469/70.] f°.

> *Ref*: HC★14704; C(Vir) 43; Stillwell S432; Goff S-478.
>
> *N.B*: The first printed commentary on Vergil.

STRABO (Strabon), *fl. 63 B.C.—A.D. 20.*

211 Geographia sive De situ orbis, libri XVI (Ed: Joannes Andreae [Giovanni
d'Andrea de' Bossi], *Bp. of Aleria, Papal Librarian, fl.* 1440–1470). Rome:
Konrad Sweynheim and Arnold Pannartz [1469]. f°.

Ref: H 15086; BMC IV 8; C 5999; Klebs 935.1; Stillwell S704; Goff S-793.

N.B: First edition. One of the finest books from a famous press. In the translation of Guarino da Verona, *c.* 1370–1460, and Gregorios Tifernas, *fl.* 1458. The manuscripts used—which were better than the Greek text used for the Aldine edition of 1516—have since been lost (Sart I 228). Entered as no. 16 on the firm's 1472 list, above the Lucanus of 1469 (Goff N-131, v. V).

THOMAS AQUINAS, *St., c.* 1225–1274.

212   Super quarto libro Sententiarum. Mainz: Peter Schoeffer, 13 June, 1469. f°.

Ref: H ★1481; BMC I 25; L-H 30; Stillwell T147; Goff T-168.

N.B: The *Sententiarum libri* of Petrus Lombardus, *Bp. of Paris, d.* 1160, was first published about 1468—*no. 143, above.* The exhaustive study of its several books formed a basis for the theology formulated by Thomas Aquinas.

VERGILIUS MARO, Publius, 70–19 B.C.

213   Opera. Rome: Konrad Sweynheim and Arnold Pannartz [1469]. f°.

Ref: Pr 3301; C(Vir) 5; Stillwell V133; Goff V-149.

N.B: Entered as no. 4 on the list of the firm's publications, preceding the entry for the Lucanus of 1469 (see vol. V. of Nicolaus de Lyra, Goff N-131). It is possible that the state of the type employed in an edition of the *Opera*, assigned to Johann Mentelin [Strasbourg, *c.* 1470, Goff V-151], may indicate its printing as early as [1469], thus making it a contender for the place of first edition.

214   Bucolica. [Cologne: Ulrich Zel, *c.* 1469.] 4°.

Ref: BMC I 182; C 6106; Pr 850; C(Vir) 112; Polain 3966; Stillwell V181; Goff V-202.

N.B: Published as a school book, as were many of the works produced by Ulrich Zel. Although written forty years before the birth of Christ, Eclogue IV foretells the coming of a child who would become a god and bring to the world the gift of peace (*cf*: HIGHET, G. *The classical tradition*, 1950, p. 72). Zel group C:1, no. 6 (BMC).

VOCABULARIUS.

215   Vocabularius ex quo. Eltvil: Nicolaus Bechtermüntze, 5 June, 1469. 4°.

Ref: BMC II 313; DeR(M) 96; Ruppel (1939) 186–189, (1947) 175–177, *fac.*

N.B: An abridged Latin-German dictionary; first issued in 1467—*no. 120, above.* In a modified version of the 1460 *Catholicon* type.

Supplementary Sections

A   Authors by Periods

B   Commentators, Editors, and Translators

C   Subject Analysis of Early Books and Broadsides

D   Typographical Analyses:
      Early Imprints of Controversial Origin
      Printers and Presses before 1470
      Printing Towns before 1470

E   Undated Imprints currently unassigned, or re-
      assigned to 1470 or later

Appendixes

A   Notes on The Gutenberg Documents:
      Subject Analysis
      Manuscript Records, 1420–1468
      Printed Statements, 1468–1499

B   Undated Imprints assigned to The Netherlands

A. Authors by Periods

Aristeas, *c. third century*, *no.* 123(137).
Aristoteles, *fourth century*, *nos.* 151–153.
Caesar, Caius Julius, *first century*, *no.* 163.
Cicero, Marcus Tullius, *first century*, *nos.* 72–75, 87, 88, 104–106. 131, 132,
 164–190.
Horatius Flaccus, Quintus, *first century*, *nos.* 77(73), 91(87).
Livius, Titus, *first century*, *nos.* 202, 203.
Vergilius Maro, Publius, *first century*, *nos.* 213, 214.

First century:
 Lucanus, Marcus Annaeus, *no.* 204.
 Plinius Secundus, Gaius, *no.* 208.
 Strabo[n], *no.* 211.

Second century:
 Albinus Platonicus, *no.* 149(150).
 Apuleius Madaurensis, *no.* 150.
 Gellius, Aulus, *no.* 193.

Third century:
 Justinus, Marcus Junianus, *no.* 201.

Fourth century:
 Donatus, Aelius, *nos.* 3, 4, 23, 33, 76, 133, 134. *See also* Appendix B,
 no. 6.
 Joannes Chrysostomus, *St.*, *nos.* 92, 93, 114, 139, 198, 199.
 Lactantius Firmianus, Caelius, *nos.* 78, 141.
 Servius Maurus, Honoratus, *no.* 210.

A—Authors by Periods (*continued*)
Fifth century:
    Augustinus, Aurelius, *nos.* 37, 81, 82, 96, 97(100), 98, 99(100), 100, 101(102), 102, 124–126.
    Hieronymus, *St.*, *nos.* 136, 137, 197.

Sixth century:
    Gregorius I, *Pont. Max.*, *no.* 195.
    Justinianus, Flavius Anicius, *no.* 140.

Ninth century:
    Rabanus Maurus (Hrabanus), *no.* 115.

Twelfth century:
    Bernardus Silvester, *no.* 159.
    Innocent III, *Pont. Max.*, *no.* 138.
    Petrus Lombardus, *no.* 143.

Thirteenth century:
    Accorso, Francesco, *no.* 121(140).
    Balbi, Giovanni, *nos.* 30, 157.
    Bonaventura, *St.*, *nos.* 85, 129.
    Bonifacius VIII, *Pont. Max.*, *nos.* 32n, 71.
    Durand, Guillaume, *nos.* 26, [67].
    Saliceto, *no.* [79b]. *See also* Appendix B, *no.* 15.
    Thomas Aquinas, *St.*, *nos.* 28, 66, 117, 118, 146, 212.

Fourteenth century:
    Andreae, Joannes, *jurist*, *no.* 70(71).
    Astesanus de Ast, *O.F.M.*, *nos.* 154, 155.
    Benedictus XII, *Pont. Max.*, *nos.* 31(32), 103(107).
    Boner, Ulrich, *nos.* 39, 54.
    Clemens V, *Pont. Max.*, 32, 107.
    Jacobus de Theramo, *no.* 63.
    Joannes XXII, *Pont. Max.*, *nos.* 34(32), 113(107).
    Matthias de Cracovia, *no.* 35.
    Nicolaus de Lyra, *no.* 142a.

Fifteenth century:
    Adolf II von Nassau, *no.* 50.
    Antonino, *St.*, *no.* 122.
    Aurbach, Johannes de, *theologian*, *no.* 156.
    Bessarion, *no.* 160.
    Brunner, Johann, *nos.* 86, 130.

Calixtus III, *Pont. Max.*, *nos.* 14, 15.

Diether von Isenberg, *nos.* 55, 56.

Friedrich III, *no.* 40.

Gerson, Jean Charlier de, *nos.* 89(90), 90, 108–112, 194.

Nicolaus V, *Pont. Max.*, *nos.* 8, 9, 10, 11.

Nider, Johann, *nos.* [68], 80*n*, 142b.

Pablo de Santa Maria, *no.* 205.

Pius II, *Pont. Max.*, *nos.* 41–49, 58a, 58b, 64, 65, 94, 206, 207.

Pontano, Ludovico, *no.* [79a]. *See also* Appendix B, *no.* 12.

Rodericus Zamorensis, *no.* 145.

Torquemada, Juan de, *no.* 119.

B.   Commentators, Editors, and Translators

Commentators

Andreae, Joannes, *jurist*,
  no. 71 (*Bonifacius* VIII)
  nos. 32, 107 (*Clemens* V)
Servius Maurus, Honoratus,
  no. 210 (*Vergilius Maro*)
Triveth, Nicolaus,
  no. 147(126) (*Augustinus, St.*)
Waleys, Thomas,
  no. 148(126) (*Augustinus, St.*)

Editors

Andreae, Joannes, *Bishop of Aleria*,
  no. 136 (*Hieronymus, St.*)
  no. 150 (*Apuleius Madaurensis*)
  no. 163 (*Caesar*)
  no. 172 (*Cicero*)
  no. 193 (*Gellius*)
  no. 202 (*Livius*)
  no. 204 (*Lucanus*)
  no. 211 (*Strabo*)

B—Editors (*continued*)

Campano, Giovanni Antonio,
    no. 203 (*Livius*)

D'Andreae de' Bossi, Giovanni. *See* Andreae, Joannes.

Lelius, Theodorus,
    no. 137 (*Hieronymus, St.*)

Tifernas, Lilius,
    no. 114 (*Joannes Chrysostomus, St.*)

Translators

Apuleius Madaurensis,
    no. 196 (*Hermes Trismegistos*)

Balbi, Pietro,
    no. 149 (*Albinus Platonicus*)

Bruni, Leonardo,
    no. 151 (*Aristoteles*)

Franciscus Aretinus,
    no. 144 (*Phalaris*)

Georgius Trapezuntius [*erroneously called* George of Trepizond],
    no. 92 (*Joannes Chrysostomus, St.*)

Gregorios Tifernas,
    no. 211 (*Strabo*)

Guarino da Verona,
    no. 211 (*Strabo*)

Palmerius, Matthias,
    no. 123 (*Aristeas*)

Tifernas, Lilius,
    no. 114 (*Joannes Chrysostomus, St.*)

Valla, Lorenzo,
    Appendix B, no. ii (*Aesopus*)

C.   Subject Analysis

In instances where a work was issued with other works, each title is entered separately, but accompanying it is the number of the first item in the compilation, enclosed in parentheses. In instances where a title has been transferred to the supplementary section entitled *Undated Imprints currently unassigned or re-assigned to 1470 or later*, the entry-number is enclosed in square brackets.

ADVERTISEMENTS: Eggestein (*41-line Bible*), no. 135.—Mentelin (*Astesanus*), no. 155; (*Pablo*), no. 205*n*.—Schoeffer (*books in stock*), no. 209; Appendix A: 2(1468).

ASTROLOGY and ASTRONOMY: Planet-table, no. 24. (*See also under* Medicine.)

BIBLE [*German*], nos. 84, 162.

BIBLE [*Latin*], nos. 1, 21, 25, 38, 51, 83, 127, 128, 161.

BIBLIA PAUPERUM, nos. 52, 53, 62, 84*n*.

CALENDARS: *For* "1448," no. 24.—*for* 1455, no. 5.—*for* 1457, no. 13.—*for* 1462, no. 36.—Cisioianus, no.16.—"Turkish calendar," no. 5

CHURCH SERVICE BOOKS and PRAYERS: Beichtbuechlein, no. 158.—Canon missae, no. 22.—Diurnale Moguntinum, no. 191.—Missale abbreviatum, no. [6].—Missale speciale, no. [7].—Passione no. 57.—Psalter (Cantica), no. 12.—Psalterium, 1457, no. 18.—Psalterium Benedictinum, 1459, no. 27.—Respice, no. 19. (*See also* Bible *and* Appendix B.)

CHURCH SYMBOLISM: Durand, nos. 26, [67].

CLASSICAL and HUMANISTIC PUBLICATIONS: Albinous Platonicus, no. 149(150).—Apuleius Madaurensis, no. 150.—Aristotle, nos. 151–153.—Bessarion, no. 160.—Caesar, no. 163.—Cicero, nos. 72–75, 87, 88, 104–106, 131, 132, 164–190.—Gellius, no. 193.—Hermes Trismegistos, no. 196 (150).—Horatius Flaccus, nos. 77(73), 91(87).—Justinus, no. 201.—Lactantius Firmianus, nos. 87, 141.—Livius, nos. 202, 203.—Lucanus, no. 204.—Phalaris, no. 144.—Pliny, *the Elder*, no. 208.—Seneca, no. [65].—Servius, no. 210.—Strabo, no. 211.—Trogus Pompeius, no. 201*n*.—Vergilius Maro, nos. 213, 214. (*See also under* Appendix B.)

COMMENTARIES: Accorso (*on Justinianus*), no. 121(140).—Andreae, Joannes, *jurist*, (*on Bonifacius VIII*), no. 71; (*on Clemens V*), nos. 32, 107.—Servius (*on Vergilius Maro*), no. 210.—Triveth (*on Augustinus*), 147(126).—Waleys (on Augustinus), no. 148(126).

CURRENT EVENTS and CONDITIONS —— 1) *Conflict over the Archbishopric of Mainz*: Adolf II von Nassau, no. 50; Diether von Isenberg, nos. 55, 56; Friedrich III, *Emperor*, no. 40; Pius II, nos. 41–46. —— 2)

C—Subject Analysis (continued)

> *Threat of Turkish Invasion*: Calixtus III, nos. 14, 15; Nicolaus V, nos. 8, 9, 10, 11; Pius II, nos. 47, 64a, 64b, 207; Warning (Eyn Manung, known as the "Turkish Calendar"), no. 5. ———— 3) *Commercial Contracts and Interest*: Nider, no. 142b.

DICTIONARIES and ETYMOLOGY: Balbi, *Catholicon*, nos. 30, 157.—Vocabularius ex quo, nos. 120, 215.

ECCLESIASTICAL LAWS: Andreae, Joannes, *jurist*, no. 70(71).—Benedictus XII, nos. 31(32), 103(107).—Bonifacius VIII, no. 71.—Clemens V., nos. 32, 107a.—Joannes XXII, nos. 34(32), 113(107a).—St. Francis, Rule of, nos. 33, 107b.

ENCYCLOPAEDIC WORKS: Pliny, *the Elder*, no. 208.—Rabanus Maurus, no. 115.

GERMAN LEGENDS and FOLKLORE: Ackermann von Böhmen, nos. 29, 61.—Boner, nos. 39, 54.—Jacobus de Theramo, no. 63.—Vier Historien, no. 60.

GRAMMAR and RHETORIC: Brunner, nos. 86, 130.—Donatus, *in 36-line Bible type*, nos. 4, 23, 33; *in 42-line Bible type*, nos. 3, 133, 134; *as first Italian imprint*, no. 76n. (*See also under* Appendix B.)

INDULGENCES: Nicolaus V, *31-line* (1454), no. 8; (1455), no. 10.—Nicolaus V, *30-line* (1454), no. 9; (1455), no. 11.—Pius II (1461), nos. 48, 49; (1462), nos. 58a, 58b; (1466), no. 94.—Radulphus, *Frater*, (1464), no. 69; (1467), no. 116.

LAW: Justianus, no. 140.—Pontano (*see* Appendix B:12.) (*See also* Ecclesiastical Laws.)

MEDICINE: Almanach für Wien, no. 36.—Calendar for 1457, no. 13.—Gerson, nos. 90, 112.—Rabanus Maurus, no. 115.—Saliceto (*see* Appendix B:15.)

NATURAL SCIENCE: Pliny, *the Elder*, no. 208.

ROMANCE: Columna, no. [132].—Pius II (Eneas Silvio Piccolomini), no. 206.

THEOLOGICAL and DEVOTIONAL WORKS: Alphabetum divini amoris, no. 80.—Antonino, *St.*, no. 122.—Aristeas, no. 123.—Astesanus de Ast, nos. 154, 155.—Augustinus, *St.*, nos. 37, 81, 82, 96–102, 124–126.—Aurbach, Johannes de, *theologian*, no. 156.—Bonaventura, *St.*, nos. 85, 129.—Exposito, no. 192.—Gerson, nos. 80n, 89(90), 108–111.—Gregorius I, no. 195.—Hieronymus, *St.*, nos. 136, 137, 197.—Innocentius III, no. 138.—Jacobus de Theramo, no. 63.—Joannes Chrysostomus, nos. 92, 93, 114, 139a–b, 198, 199, 200(122).—Matthias de Cracovia, no. 35.—Nicolaus de Hanapis, no. 85n.—Nicolaus de Lyra, no. 142a.—Nider, nos. [68], 80 *n*.—

Pablo de Santa Maria, no. 205.—Passione di Cristo, no. 57.—Petrus Lombardus, no. 143, 212*n*.—Precatio, no. 17.—Sánchez de Arévalo, no. 145.—Sieben Freuden Mariae, no. 59.—Thomas Aquinas, *St.*, nos. 28, 66, 117, 118, 146, 212.—Torquemada, no. 119. (*See also* Ecclesiastical Laws *above*; *and under* Appendix B.)

VERSE: Brunner, nos. 86, 130.—Cisioianus, no. 16.—Eyn Manung . . . wider die Durken, no. 5.—Horatius Flaccus, nos. 77(73), 91(87).—Sibyllenbuch (Weltergericht), no. 2.—Vergilius Maro, nos. 213, 214. (*See also* Appendix B:9.)

D. Typographical Analyses of Imprints before 1470

D:1 EARLY IMPRINTS OF CONTROVERSIAL ORIGIN

Bible, 42-line ("Gutenberg Bible"), *no. 1*. —— Bible, 36-line, *no. 25*. —— "Calendar of 1448" (Planet table), *no. 24*. —— Catholicon, 1460, *no. 30*. —— Cisioianus, *no. 16*. —— Donatus [42-line Bible type, 1st state], *no. 3*; [36-line Bible type, 1st state], *no. 4*; [36-line Bible type, 2nd state], *no. 23*. —— Missale abbreviatum, *no.* [6]. —— Missale speciale, *no.* [7]. — Sibyllenbuch, *no. 2*. *In 42-line Bible type*: nos. 1, 3, 9, 11, 12, 133, 134*n*. —— *In 36-line Bible type*: nos. 25, 2, 4, 5, 8, 10, 13, 14, 15, 16, 17, 19, 20, 21, 23, 24, 29, 33b, 39, 52, 53, 54, 61, 62, 63. — *In Catholicon type*: nos. 30, 28, 35, 48, 58b, 120, 215. — *Unlocalized imprints*: nos. 36, 57, 59, 138. —— *Unassigned or reassigned imprints*: nos. [6], [7], [65], [67], [68], [79a], [79b], [132b]. (*See also* APPENDIX B: Undated Imprints assigned to The Netherlands.)

D:2 PRINTERS AND PRESSES BEFORE 1470

The place and date of the earliest extant imprint are cited after the printer's name. In instances where a work was issued with others, the entry-number is followed by that of the compilation, in parentheses.

Bechtermüntze, Heinrich, *Eltvil*, 1467: *no. 120*.

Bechtermüntze, Nicolaus, *Eltvil*, 1469: *no. 215*.

Eggestein, Heinrich, [*Strasbourg*, 1466]: *nos. 83, 85, 127, 135, 161, 162*.

Fust, Johann, [*Mainz, c. 1452?*, 1466/67]: *nos. 1, 82, 86*. See also Appendix A, 1455.

Fust, Johann, and Peter Schoeffer, [*Mainz*] 1457: *nos. 18, 22, 26, 27, 31, 32*,

D:2—Printers and Presses (continued)

34(32), 37, 40, 41, 42, 43, 44, 46, 47, 49, 50, 51, 55, 56, 58a, 64a, 64b, 69, 70(71), 71, 73, 75(73), 77(73), 87, 88(87), 91(87).

Gutenberg, Johann, [*Mainz, 1450/55*] (?): *nos.* 1, 3, 28, 30, 35, 48, 58b. *See also above, under* D:1 EARLY IMPRINTS OF CONTROVERSIAL ORIGIN: *in* 42-line Bible type; *in* 36-line Bible type; *and in* Catholicon type.

Han, Ulrich, *Rome, 1467: nos.* 119, 131, 144, 164, 166(174), 167(176), 173, 174, 176, 180, 182(174), 183(176), 184, 186(174), 187(176), 188(184), 189(176) 190, 201, 203, 210.

Henricus Ariminensis, Printer of. See Reyser, Georg.

Johann von Speier, [*Venice*] 1469: *nos.* 170, 171, 208.

Lotharius, Printer of: no. 138.

Mentelin, Johann [*Strasbourg, n.a.* 1461]: *nos.* 38, 66, 81, 84, 92, 94, 124, 126, 147(126), 148(126), 151, 152(151), 153(151), 154, 155, 197, 205.

Passione di Cristo, Printer of: nos. 57, 59.

Pfister, Albrecht, [*Bamberg, c.* 1460]: *nos.* 29, 33b, 39, 52, 53, 54, 60, 61, 62, 63.

R-printer. See Rusch, Adolf.

Reyser, Georg, [*Strasbourg, n.a.* 1468]: *no.* 143.

Riessinger, Sixtus [*Rome,* 1468/70]: *nos.* 123(137), 137.

Ruppel, Berthold, [*Basel, c.* 1468]: *nos.* 128, 142a, 195.

Rusch, Adolf, [*Strasbourg,* 1467]: *no.* 115.

Schoeffer, Peter, *Mainz, 1467: nos.* 103(107), 107, 113(107), 118, 121(140), 130, 133, 134, 140, 158, 191, 194, 209, 212. *See also* Fust and Schoeffer.

Sweynheim, Konrad, and Arnold Pannartz, [*Subiaco,* 1465]: *nos.* 74, 76, 78, 96. — *Rome,* 1467: *nos.* 104, 125, 132a, 136, 141, 145, 149(150), 150, 160, 163, 165(175), 168, 169(179), 172, 175, 177(168), 178(179), 179, 181(175), 185(175), 193, 196(150), 202, 204, 211, 213.

Zainer, Günther, *Augsburg,* [14]68: *nos.* 129, 156, 157, 159, 192.

Zel, Ulrich, [*Cologne, c.* 1465]: *nos.* 72, 80, 89(90), 90, 93, 97(100), 98, 99(100), 100, 101(102), 102, 105, 106, 108a(112), 108b, 109(111), 110 [*3 titles*], 111, 112, 114, 116, 117, 122, 139a(122), 139b, 142b, 146, 198, 199, 206, 207, 214. [*For* "Zel group" *see under* Abbreviations, Symbols, and Terms.]

D:3   PRINTING TOWNS BEFORE 1470

D:3a   THE FIRST PRINTED STATEMENTS OF PLACE, PRINTER, OR DATE

Introduced:		*Place*	*Printer*	*Date*
[1450/55]	Mainz	no. 30, *in 1460*	no. 18, *in 1457*	no. 18, *in 1457*

Introduced:		*Place*	*Printer*	*Date*
[1458/59]	Bamberg	no. 39, *in 1461*	no. 60, *in 1462*	no. 39, *in 1461*
[*n.a.* 1461]	Strasbourg	. . . .	. . . .	. . . .
[*c.* 1465]	Cologne	. . . .	no. 93, *in 1466*	no. 93, *in 1466*
1465	Subiaco	no. 78, *in 1465*	. . . .	no. 78, *in 1465*
1467	Rome	no. 104, *in 1467*	no. 104, *in 1467*	no. 104, *in 1467*
1467	Eltvil	no. 120, *in 1467*	no. 120, *in 1467*	no. 120, *in 1467*
1468	Augsburg	no. 129, *in 1468*	no. 129, *in 1468*	no. 129, *in 1468*
[*c.* 1468]	Basel	. . . .	. . . .	. . . .
1469	Venice	no. 171, *in 1469*	no. 170, *in 1469*	no. 170, *in 1469*

D:3b COMPLETE PRINTED STATEMENTS OF PLACE, PRINTER, AND DATE

[1450/55] Mainz, *nos.* 51, *in 1462*; 71; 107a; 118; 140; 212.

[1458/59] Bamberg, *no.* 60, *in 1462*.

[*n.a.* 1461] Strasbourg, [*sine nota*].

[*c.* 1465] Cologne, *no.* 93, *in 1466* [*printer and date only*].

1465 Subiaco, *no.* 78, *in 1465* [*place and date only*].

1467 Rome, *nos.* 104, *in 1467*; 119; 125; 131; 141; 145; 172; 190; 204.

1467 Eltvil, *nos.* 120, *in 1467*; 215.

1468 Augsburg, *nos.* 129, *in 1468*; 156; 157.

[*c.* 1468] Basel, [*sine nota*].

1469 Venice, *nos.* 171, *in 1469*; 208.

D:3c PLACES OF PRINTING

Mainz: nos. 1, 2, 3, 4, 5, 8, 9, 10, 11, 12, 13, 14, 15, 16, 17, 18, 19, 20, 21, 22, 23a–d, 24, 26, 27, 28, 30, 31(32), 32, 33a, 33b, 34(32), 35, 37, 40, 41, 42, 43, 44, 46, 47, 48, 49, 50, 51, 55, 56, 58a–b, 64a–b, 65, 69, 70(71), 71, 73, 75(73), 77(73), 82, 86, 87, 88(87), 91(87), 103(107), 107, 107b(107), 113(107), 118, 121(140), 130, 133, 134, 140, 158, 191, 194, 209, 212.

Bamberg: nos. 25, 29, 33b, 39, 52, 53, 54, 60, 61, 62, 63.

Strasbourg: nos. 38, 66b, 81, 83, 84, 85, 92, 94, 115, 124, 126, 127, 135, 143, 147(126), 148(126), 151, 152(151), 153(151), 154, 155, 161, 162, 197, 205.

Cologne: nos. 72, 80, 89(90), 90, 93, 97(100), 98, 99(100), 100, 101(102), 102, 105, 106, 108a(112), 108b, 109(111), 110[3 titles], 111, 112, 114, 116, 117, 122, 139a(122), 139b, 142b, 146, 198, 199, 206, 207, 214—*see also no.* 200.

Subiaco: nos. 74, 76, 78, 96.

D:3—Printing Towns (continued)

Rome: *nos.* 104, 119, 123(137), 125, 131, 132a, 136, 137, 141, 144, 145, 149(150), 150, 160, 163, 164, 165(175), 166(174), 167(176), 168, 169(179), 172, 173, 174, 175, 176, 177(168), 178(179), 179, 180, 181(175), 182(174), 183(176), 184, 185(175), 186(174), 187(176), 188(184), 189(176), 190, 193, 196(150), 201, 202, 203, 204, 210, 211, 213.

Eltvil: *nos.* 120, 215.

Augsburg: *nos.* 129, 156, 157, 159, 192.

Basel: *nos.* 128, 142, 195.

Venice: *nos.* 170, 171, 208.

[*See also* APPENDIX B: *Undated imprints assigned to The Netherlands.*]

E. Undated Imprints currently unassigned, or re-assigned to 1470 or later

Transferred from 1454

MISSALE ABBREVIATUM.

[6] —— [Basel: Printer of the *Missale speciale*, before 1474.] f°. 72 ff.

> *Ref*: DeR(M) 64; Ruppel (1939) 169, (1947) 159; Stevenson (1967) 71, 167, *etc.*
> *Cop*: Benedictine Abbey of Saint Paul, Carinthia, *unique.*
> *N.B*: Presumably issued as a Missal for itinerant or personal use. Printed in the same type as the *Missale speciale*, no. [7] below, but with bibliographical variations in addition to its shortened form. Although not having been subjected through the years to as meticulous a study as the former, it is searchingly discussed by Stevenson in his 1967 monograph on the *Missale speciale*, where in presenting 1473 as the presumable date of publication, he submits that "the *Abbreviatum* was issued probably in the summer and the *Speciale* by the fall of that year."
> *Mon*: UNTERKIRCHER, Franz. *Das Missale abbreviatum von St. Paul* (in *Das Antiquariat*, Vienna, October, 1954); with reproductions.

MISSALE SPECIALE (*formerly called* Missale speciale Constantiense).

[7] —— [Basel?; Eponymous press, in small 1457-Psalter type, *early state*, before 1474.] f°. 192 ff.

> *Ref*: DeR(M) 63; Stevenson (1967) 170–175, *etc.*; Goff M-655.
> *Cop*: Zurich; Munich; Augsburg—New York (PML).
> *N.B*: Presumably issued for the use of churches and monastic chapels. The question of the origin and date of the *Missale speciale* has been the cause of excited debate at the turn of the century and at intervals during the present century, the hypo-

thetical date-assignments ranging from 1445 to 1490. The controversy continued intermittently until, in the 1960s, it assumed new life and was approached from new angles, as the result of the purchase, announced in 1954 by the Pierpont Morgan Library, of one of the four copies now known to be extant.

[With regard to the earlier period of the controversy, see SCHMIDT-KÜNSEMÜLLER, F. A. *Der Streit um das Missale speciale, ein Forschungsbericht* (p. 51–89 in OHLY, K. and W. KRIEG, ed. *Aus der Welt Bibliothekars: Festschrift für Rudolf Juchhoff*, Cologne, 1961), which lists seventy or more papers issued during 1896–1960. For a selective list of those published during 1898–1962, see the Third Census of *Incunabula in American Libraries* (Goff M-655). For a summary of the various arguments, *see* ALTMANN, Ursula. *Das Missale Speciale (Constantiense) und der Gesamtkatalog der Wiegendrucke* (p. 403–426 in *Deutsche Staatsbibliothek: Vorträge Berichte und Dokumente zur Dreihundertjahrfeier 23–28 October 1961*), Berlin, 1962.]

Mon: GELDNER, Ferdinand. *Das "Missale speciale" (bisher "Constantiense" genannt), liturgie- und typengeschichtlich neu gesehen* (p. 596–604 in *Archiv für Geschichte des Buchwesens* II 1960). GERARDY, Theo. *Die Wasserzeichen des mit Gutenbergs kleiner Psaltertype gedruckten Missale speciale* (p. 13–22 in *Papiergeschichte* X 1960); *Zur Datierung des mit Gutenbergs kleiner Psaltertype gedruckten Missale speciale* (col. 399–415 in *Archiv für Geschichte des Buchwesens* V 1963). PICCARD, Gerhard. *Die Datierung des Missale speciale (Constantiense) durch seine Papiermarken* (p. 571–584 in *Archiv für Geschichte des Buchwesens* II 1960). STEVENSON, Allan. *Paper evidence and the Missale speciale* (p. 94–105 in *Gutenberg Jahrbuch* 1962); *The Problem of the Missale speciale*, London, 1967. [In the latter, a monograph of 400 pages, Stevenson provides a meticulous survey of the subject as a whole, and presents cause for considering that the paper, on which the *Missale speciale* was printed, was manufactured early in 1473 and the book itself produced later in the same year, at Basel, possibly at the press of Johann Meister. The question of identification is still, however, a fluid one. According to recent correspondence, Dr. CURT F. BÜHLER has in hand a paper on the relevance of watermarks to date-assignment; and another about to come out in the *Papers* of the Bibliographical Society of America applying careful analysis to the question whether or not the *Missale speciale*, which does not include the Office for the Feast of the Presentation of the Blessed Virgin Mary (promulgated 30 May 1468) was printed prior to that date. [For earlier discussion by Dr. Bühlur, *see* BSA. *Papers*, 1956, p. 370–5; The Book Collector, VI, 1957, p. 253–8; The Library, March 1959, p. 1–10.]

Transferred from 1463

SENECA, Lucius Annaeus, *c.* 4 B.C.–A.D. 65.

[65] De quattuor virtutibus. [Paris: Petrus Caesaris and Johannes Stol, *c.* 1473–1475.]

   Ref: Oates 2894–2895.

   N.B: Originally a "ghost-entry" which, owing to a fraudulent colophon in manuscript, in a copy at the University of Glasgow, was erroneously entered in Cop III 5351 and DeR(M) 80 under the imprint: [Mainz: Johann Fust and Peter Schoeffer, 1463]. Actually an imperfect copy of Oates 2894–2895. *See* GOFF, F. R. *Falsified Dates in Certain Incunabula* (in *Homage to a Bookman* [Hans P. Kraus], Berlin, 1967, p. 142); GASKELL, P. (In *The Library*, Ser. 5, vol. XIX, 1964, p. 200–201, with plate). Authorship questioned.

Transferred from 1464

DURAND, Guillaume (Durandus; Guillelmus Duranti), *Bishop of Mende,* 1237–1296.

[67] Rationale divinorum officiorum. [Strasbourg: The R-Printer (Adolph Rusch), "1464," not after 1474.] f°.

   Ref: GW 9102; H *6461; BMC I 60; Stillwell D329; Goff D-405.

   N.B: Second edition. First printed at Mainz in 1459. The date 1464, by which it is usually known and which is inscribed in Roman numerals in a copy at Basel, has been shown to be an error for 1474. [For discussion, see E. von Rath's essay in *Beiträge zur Inkunabelkunde*, 1938; V. Scholderer's essay on *Adolf Rusch and the earliest roman types* (in *The Library*, June 1939); and S. Morison's *Early humanistic script and the first roman type* (p. 1–29 in *The Library*, 1943).] Before Adolph Rusch had been identified as the head of this firm, he was designated as the R-Printer, because of a strangely formed capital "R" that is characteristic of this press.

    Formerly this edition of Durand ranked as the first book printed in roman type—a simple but handsome type-design reminiscent of early Roman inscriptions. Because of the error in its dating, it has since given place to a Rabanus Maurus (no. 115 below) assigned to 1467, as the first Rusch imprint and probably the first book in roman type.

NIDER, Johann (Hansen Nÿder), *Dominican,* 1380–1438.

[68] Praeceptorium divinae legis, sive Expositio decalogi. [Basel: Berthold Ruppel, "1464," not after 1474.] f°.

   Ref: H *11782; BMC III 715; Polain 2872; Stillwell N172; Goff N-196.

   N.B: For several years this stood accepted as the first Basel imprint, following the discovery in 1932 by Mr. Fritz Finkenstaedt of a rubricator's date reading "M°cccc°lxiiij" [1464], in the Rosenthal copy at Munich. The authenticity of the rubricator's inscription was submitted to expert scrutiny, and it has never been questioned. But in a subsequent study of the book, Dr. Scholderer found certain features known only in Ruppel imprints of much later date. Dr. Scholderer therefore submits in his *The beginnings of printing at Basel* (p. 50 in *The*

Library, 5th Ser., III, 1948/49) that an "x" may have accidentally been omitted in the writing of the date, which (with the "x" supplied) would then read "M°cccc°lxxiiij" [1474].

It is believed that the printer, Berthold Ruppel, may have been the Bechtolff von Hanau whom Gutenberg sent to report to him the proceedings on the occasion when Fust in November 1455 had sworn to the veracity of his financial claims against him. (For early Basel imprints as contenders for priority, *see nos.* 128, 142, and 195, *above*.)

Transferred from 1465

PONTANO, Ludovico (Ludovicus Pontanus), *jurist*, 1409–1439.

[79a] Singularia in causis criminalibus. [*See* APPENDIX B: Undated imprints assigned to The Netherlands, no. B:12.]

SALICETO (Guglielmo Salicito), 1210–1277.

[79b] De salute corporis. [*See* Appendix B: Undated imprints assigned to The Netherlands, no. B:15.]

Transferred from 1468

COLUMNA, Guido de (Guido della Colonna), *thirteenth century*.

[132b] Kronika trojanska [*Czech*]. [Prague or Plzeň: anonymous printer, "1468," 1476/78?]. 8°.

> *Ref*: Highet (CT) 50–55.
> *N.B*: The so-called "Trojan chronicle," a romance of chivalry written about the end of the thirteenth century and recounting the story of the destruction of ancient Troy. Based on *Le roman de Troie* by Benoît de Sainte-Maure, *fl*. 1160. Although the date 1468 appears at the end of the text, its relevance to this volume has been questioned on the ground that a manuscript at the monastery of Osek near Duchcov, from which this may have been copied, is dated 1468. The presence of certain characters which appeared in the *Agenda Pragensis*, issued somewhat later at Plzeň has raised the question as to whether the "Trojan chronicle" may have been printed somewhat later than 1468.
> *Mon*: HORAK, Frantisek. *Pět století českeho knihtisku* [Five hundred years of Czech printing], Prague, 1968, p. 116–117, 160–162, *fac*.

DONATUS, Aelius. *See note under no. 134 (p. 40, above).*

The Gutenberg Documents:
Notes on the
Manuscript Records
1420–1468

The dates refer to the documents which are cited below, in chronological order.

Birth, *circa* 1399
    1420

Decease and Estate
    1468

Exile from Mainz
    1430

Family and Kinsmen
    1420
    1427
    1433
    1434
    1448

Inheritance and Annuities
    1420
    1427/28
    1430
    1433
    1434
    1436/37
    1442
    1453–55

Lawsuits
    1436–37 (Breach of promise)
    1439 (Dritzehen)
    1455 (Fust—Helmasperger
        Instrument)

Loans and Interest
    1441
    1442
    1444
    1444–57
    1448
    1455
    1461/62
    1468

Partners and Associates
    1439 (Dritzehen, Riffe and
        Heilmann)
    1439 (Dünne)
    1442 (Brechter)

    1444 (Heilmann)
    1444 (Brechter)
    1455 (Fust)
    1455 (Gunther, Bechtolff v. Hanau,
        and Keffer)
    1468 (Humery)

Personal Activities
  At Strasbourg
    1434–44
  At Mainz
    1430
    1448
    1453
    1457
    1458
    1467–68

Professional Career
  As Master-goldsmith
    1444
  As Inventor of Printing
    1439
    1455
    1458
    1470–99   [*Printed*]
  As Printer and Type-cutter
    1439
    1455
    1458
    1468
    1468–99   [*Printed*]

Status and Rank
    1430
    1436–40
    1443
    1443–44
    1444
    1465

Taxes
    1436
    1443
    1443/44

Appendix A

Notes on Documentary Sources and Statements relative to Johann Gensfleisch zur Laden zu Gutenberg, *c.* 1399–1467/68

1) *The Manuscript Records, 1420–1468*

The numerals in parentheses or brackets accompanied by the initials F, M, or R refer respectively to FUHRMANN, O. W. *Gutenberg and the Strasbourg documents of 1439*, New York, 1940; McMURTRIE, D. C. *The Gutenberg documents with translations of the texts based with authority on the compilation of Dr. Karl Schorbach*, New York, 1941; and RUPPEL, Aloys. *Johannes Gutenberg, sein Leben und sein Werk*, Berlin, 1947.

For a recension of these documents, see SCHORBACH, Karl. *Die urkundlichen Nachrichten über Johann Gutenberg* (in *Beiheft zum Centralblatt für Bibliothekswesen*, 1900, VIII, no. 23); and his *Neue Strassburgische Gutenbergfunde* (in *Gutenberg-Jahrbuch*, 1926). For English translations and comments on legal points in the fifteenth century, see McMURTRIE. Further details regarding the present location of transcripts are listed in RUPPEL (1947) 18–20. [See also RUPPEL, Aloys. *Die Technik Gutenbergs und ihre Vorstufen*, 2nd., 1961.]

The term *Collectio Wenckeriana*, which is occasionally cited below, refers to the notes and transcripts in the Municipal Archives and at St. Thomas Chapter at Strasbourg as collected by Jacob Wencker, 1669–1743.

In instances where originals have been lost, as is true of many of these documents, the texts are known through copies or secondary records, which some scholars accept as authentic and others believe are open to question. It will be noted that, in quotations given below, the names frequently appear in the variety of forms and spellings characteristic of place and period.

75

1420   An instrument of 1420 now lost, but summarized in a seventeenth-century record at Darmstadt, relates to "legal disputes and errors" concerning Friele zur Laden, his brother Henchen [Johann], and their brother-in-law, Clas Vitzthumb (M 48). This would seem to indicate that the brothers were of legal age when the instrument was drawn, for which reason Johann Gutenberg's birth is computed as 1399 or earlier. Since Gutenberg's father had died in 1419, the document is supposed to relate to the settling of his estate. According to the *Genealogie des Mainzer Geschlechtes Gänsfleisch* (p. 65-131 in *Festschrift zum fünfhundertjährigen Geburtstage von Johann Gutenberg.* Otto Hartwig, *ed.* Mainz, 1900), Gutenberg's parents were married in 1386, and Johann was the youngest of three children, the others being Friele and Else, the wife of Clas Vitzthumb. (M 26-31) [R 18:1]

[1427– Two sixteenth-century transcripts in the city library at Mainz and the
1428]   archives of Würzburg (M 49-52) indicate the former existence of a manuscript relative to the transfer of an annuity, which had hitherto been allotted to "the brothers Frielen and Hengi(n)s [Johann], sons of the late Friele zu Gudenberg." The assignment of the dates rests on the fact that neighboring items in the Mainz volume are of those years. The presiding judge is not known in office after 1434. (M 50) [R 18:2]

1430   A statement in the *Schuldbuch* of Mainz (lost after the publication of
Jan. 16 its text, by Johann David Köhler in 1741) records on 16 January, 1430 the re-arrangement of an annuity, apparently paid by the city of Mainz to Gutenberg, according to which his mother would henceforth be paid one half as long as her son lived. (M 54, 55) [R 18:3]

1430   In an Act of Reconciliation by Konrad, Archbishop of Mainz, pro-
Mar. 28 claiming the reorganization of the government of Mainz and inviting the return of certain members of patrician families then in exile, "Henchin zu Gudenberg" is listed among those not at present in Mainz, but hereby permitted to return. The text of the original document, now lost, is known through a transcript in a fifteenth-century codex in the Stadtbibliothek at Frankfurt. (M 56) [R 18:4]

1433   A seventeenth-century chronicle at Darmstadt, quoting from a
Aug. 2 document now lost, records the dividing of the estate of Gutenberg's mother between the brothers "Friele and Henne Gensfleisch,"

and their sister and her husband. Witnesses: . . . [4 names, including] . . . Peter Gelthauss. (M 69) [R 18:5]

1434
Mar. 14   At the request of the Council of Strasbourg, "Johann Gensfleisch" releases his legal claim against the Clerk of Mainz, whom he had had arrested for the non-payment of annuity interest due Gutenberg from the city of Mainz, which sum of "three hundred and ten good Rhenish *gulden*" was to have been paid before Pentecost at *zum Lamparten*, the estate of Gutenberg's cousin, Ort Geldthuss, near Oppenheim (M 72–73). [From an eighteenth-century transcript of the original Strasbourg manuscript, found by Dr. Karl Schorbach and recorded by him in *Gutenberg Festschrift zur Feier des 25-jährigen Bestehens des Gutenbergs Museums in Mainz*. Mainz, 1925, p. 134–143 (M 71).] [R 18:6]

1434
May 30   According to two eighteenth-century transcripts at Darmstadt, from a codex now lost, the city of Mainz on 30 May, 1434, reached an agreement with "Hengin Gudenberg, son of the late Friele Genssefleisch" whereby an annuity of 14 *gulden* registered to "Friele, his brother, a resident of Eltville," should henceforth—with a reduction of 2 *gulden*—be paid Hengin on a semi-annual basis. (M 74) [R 18:7]

1436–
1437   In a Mainz account-book for 1436–1437, now at Würzburg (M 77), several brief entries relate to Gutenberg, the most important of which are that 35 *gulden* "on account of all overdue annuities," and 10 *gulden* "on account of the late judge Leheymer" were paid "Clais Victzdum" on behalf of "Henne Gennsefleisse, called Gudenberg" at the time of the Frankfurt Fair of last Lent and of the "Annunciatio Mariae," respectively. (M 79) [R 18:8]

1436–
1440   "Hans Gutenberg of Mainz" is listed in an eighteenth-century Wencker transcript of the tax-register of Strasbourg for 1436–1440, as having paid a wine tax on 9 July, 1439 (M 82) and as being registered as "non-affiliated," *i.e.*, not belonging to a local guild nor to the local aristocracy. (M 81) [R 18:11]

1436–
1437   Two documents, in which "Hansse Gensfleisch of Mainz, called Gutenberg" is shown to be involved in a breach of promise suit,

and in the course of it to have been fined provisionally in the ecclesiastical court of Strasbourg, for using defamatory language (M 87). This testimony, which rested on Schöflin's account in his *Vindiciae Typographicae*, 1760, was suspect as a forgery and the subject of controversy for over a century. But Schorbach in 1926 managed to verify the actuality of such a lawsuit, through two notes written prior to 1743 and contained in Wencker's *Collectanea*, a codex in the archives of St. Thomas Chapter at Strasbourg, comprising excerpts from early documents, or Wencker's notes regarding them (M 86, 87). The outcome is not known beyond the facts that the lady in question is subsequently listed under her maiden name among contributors to a defense fund, *etc.*, and that Gutenberg never became a citizen of Strasbourg, as would have been his status had they married. (M 91, 92) [R 18:9–10]

1439
Dec. 12

A lawsuit brought against Gutenberg on 12 December, 1439, by Jerge and Claus Dritzehen would seem to indicate that Gutenberg had for some time been in partnership with Andres Dritzehen, Hanns Riffe, and Andres Heilmann. Following Dritzehen's death, his brothers now claimed his place in the partnership, or a return of such money as he had invested in it (M 107).

The purpose of the firm is not stated, and the depositions of the many witnesses are vague and jumbled. There are, however, references to the making of *Spiegeln* for sale during the Aix-la-Chapelle pilgrimage (M 112), mention of the purchase of lead (M 121), and a recurring theme regarding "four pieces" that were to be taken apart by releasing two hand-screws and laid "upon the press apart from each other," so that mourners coming to the Dritzehen house "cannot know what it is" (M 104, 105). And the deposition of one witness, "Hanns Dünne the goldsmith," yields the significant statement that about three years prior to that time he had received from Gutenberg approximately a hundred *gulden*, for what pertained to printing alone—*alleine das zu dem trucken gehöret* (M 101).

In summarizing the testimony, the Master and Council of Strasbourg refer to Gutenberg as having said that he had taught Andres Dritzehen "to polish stones" (M 122) and had taught his three partners an art to be used for their mutual profit during the pilgrimage (M 122). When the pilgrimage was postponed for a year, they had arranged with Gutenberg "to teach them all his arts . . . and not to keep anything secret from them" (M 123). In the verdict rendered, Gutenberg was instructed to give the Dritzehen brothers 15 *gulden*, upon the receipt of which they should have no further claim against him. (M 126) [R 19:1–2]

The original records were lost in 1793 and 1870, but the texts had already appeared in Schöflin in 1760 and in Laborde in 1840. With regard to this controversial lawsuit, see also Hessels, 1882; Schorbach, 1892, 1900; McMurtrie, 1941. For the original Alsatian text as given in Schöflin, with translations in English, modern German, and Laborde's French version together with notes and comments, see Fuhrmann (F 156–236).

The term *four pieces* is used by witnesses in the 1439 lawsuit, with regard an implement which Gutenberg had insisted should be taken apart so that persons coming to the funeral of his deceased partner would not "see or comprehend" what it was (F 157, 159, 165). According to the diagram given in Fuhrmann (F 75), this refers to a four-piece type-casting mould comprising two rectangular metal blocks of equal length fastened together with screws, but holding between them two shorter metal blocks, which before the whole was fastened in place were free to be moved toward one another or away. Thus a plane-parallel channel was produced for the shank of the type, with the two opposite slides adjustable to the letter-width of whatever matrix might be inserted before the whole was clamped together. For discussion of this and other interpretations of the *four pieces*, see Fuhrmann (F 75, 101–140).

1441
Jan. 12,
etc.

In a particularly involved and confusing document drawn up in the court at Strasbourg, Luthold von Ramstein and "Johann called Gensefleisch, otherwise named Gutenberg of Mainz, resident at Strasbourg" stand as surety and co-debtors for the loan of 100 *gulden* to Johann Karle, knight, by St. Thomas Chapter—thus showing Gutenberg's financial status to have been acceptable and sound at the time. The document's special interest lies in the way it circumvents the medieval law banning the payment and receipt of interest (which nevertheless was to be paid at the rate of five pounds a year), and in its recital of the woeful consequences in the event of default, by which means St. Thomas Chapter sought to protect itself (M 131–134)—the penalties for the co-debtors and their heirs being excommunication, property forfeiture, and loss of the right to appeal under canon or civil law.

[*Original lost; known through a transcript in the "Salbuch," 1343–1502, in the archives of St. Thomas Chapter (M 127) at Strasbourg.*]
[R 19:3]

1442
Nov. 17

"Johannes called Gensefleische" and Martin Brechter [Brehter] appear on 17 November, 1442, before the court at Strasbourg and contract a loan for Gutenberg of eighty pounds of Strasbourg *denarii*, from St. Thomas Chapter. Upon this he agreed to pay four pounds annually "at the feast of the sainted Bishop Martin" (M 144), giving as surety the annuity of 10 *gulden* bequeathed him by his granduncle, Johann Leymeyer [*see 1436–1437, above*] and payable by the city of Mainz (M 144, 141). The contract follows the general pattern of that of 1441, above, in concealing the payment of interest and imposing devastating penalties upon the co-debtors and their heirs in the event of default in payment.

[*Original lost in the burning of the municipal library at Strasbourg in 1870; known through a transcript in the "Salbuch," 1343–1502, in the archives of St. Thomas Chapter (M 140) at Strasbourg.*] [R 19:4]

1443
Feb. 24

An excerpt from the *Helbeling* taxbook of Strasbourg, quoted in the *Collectanea Wenckeriana*, lists "Hans Guttenberg" under the affiliated aristocracy [*i.e.*, of patrician status but not a citizen of Strasbourg] and states that on St. Matthew's Day, 1443, he paid a tax for two persons including himself (M 150, 151).

[*Original taxbook lost; Wencker excerpts in archives of St. Thomas Chapter at Strasbourg.*] [R 19:5]

[1443–
1444?]

In a tax levied against residents of Strasbourg for the defense of the city, presumably against the Armagnacs, who attacked it in 1443 and 1444, Gutenberg is listed among the *Constofeler*, the local aristocracy, and is taxed for half a horse—"Hanns Guttenberg, 1/2 horse" (M 153).

[*Original list in Strasbourg archives (M 152).*] [R 19:6]

[1444,
Jan. 22]

In a Strasbourg document assigned to 1444, listing persons eligible for military service, "Hansse Gutenberg . . . Andres Heilman" are listed among "master-goldsmiths and painters and saddlers and harness-makers," associated members of the guild (M 155).

[*Original list in Strasbourg archives.*] [R 19:7]

1444
Mar. 12   An entry from the *Helbeling* taxbook indicates that Gutenberg paid
1 *gulden* on St. Gregory's Day, 1444 (M 151). [Original taxbook
lost; known through an excerpt in the *Collectanea Wenckeriana*, in
St. Thomas' archives, a collection compiled by the Strasbourg
archivist, Jakob Wencker (*d.* 1743); printed by Schöpflin in 1760
(M 84).] Incidentally, this is the last definite day when Gutenberg
is known to have been in Strasbourg. (But see 1453–1455 below,
for annuities paid to Gutenberg by the city of Strasbourg during
those years.) [R 19:8]

1444–
1458,   A series of codices in St. Thomas' archives at Strasbourg record that
etc.   Gutenberg paid the annual interest of four *Pfund* due the Chapter,
in the years 1444/45, 1445/46, 1449/50, 1452/53, 1456/57 [together
with his co-debtor, Martin Brechter], and 1457/58. The account
books for the intervening years have been lost, but it has been
pointed out that no records of unpaid interest have been carried
forward. This would seem to indicate that the debt contracted by
Gutenberg and Brechter on 17 November, 1442 [see above] was
paid through 1457/58.
    [*Originals extant, as indicated* (M 158).] [*See also* R 19:9;
20:2–6.]

1448
Oct. 17   In the record of a loan contracted before the court of Mainz by
Arnold Gelthuss zur Echtzeler on 17 October, 1448, it is stated that
"Henn Genssefleisch who is called Gudenbergk" was present and
that he promised to redeem the 150 *gulden* borrowed by Gelthuss
on his behalf, and meanwhile to pay seven and a half *gulden* annually. The contract resorts to similar subterfuge regarding the
payment of interest, but does not include the stringent penalties
stipulated in the St. Thomas loan of 12 January, 1441 [*see above*].
Four persons named Gelthuss figure in matters connected with
Gutenberg. In one instance, that in which Gutenberg himself
speaks, on 14 March, 1434 [*q.v.*], he refers to "my cousin Ort
Gelthuss" (M 72). The genealogical chart in Dr. Ruppel's volume
shows Gutenberg's grandmother to have been the daughter of
Johann zur jungen Aben zum Gelthuss. It therefore seems probable
that the Arnold Gelthuss who stood as surety in the present loan,
and Adam Gelthuss (who composed the epitaph quoted under 1499
in Appendix A) were kinsmen of Gutenberg.
    [*Known through a transcript of the original, certified by the civil*

court of Mainz, 23 August, 1503; in the municipal library at Mainz (M 160–166).] [R 19:10]

1453–
1455

In a record of annuity payments made by the city of Strasbourg to citizens of Mainz and Frankfurt, three payments were made in 1453–1455 to "Johann Guttemberg, called Gensefleich." Two of these payments were made to Johann Bunne or his wife, as agents for Gutenberg. The third, that of 1455, was paid to Gutenberg himself at the "Lenten fair" (M 173). The place is open to question. Strasbourg has been suggested. But since, in a payment to Gutenberg from the city of Mainz in 1436/37 [*q.v.*], a receipt for it was given by his brother-in-law, Clais Victzdum at "the Frankfurt Fair of last Lent," it is possible that Gutenberg may have received the current payment at Frankfurt.

[*Records extant, in the archives of Strasbourg. Discovered by Schorbach in 1918 and published by him in the GUTENBERG FEST-SCHRIFT, 1925 (M 172).*] [R 19:12]

1453
July 3

On 3 July, 1453, "Johann Gudenberg" was present at Mainz as one of five witnesses to a contract made with regard to a future bequest by Hans Schuchman, to the nuns' convent of St. Clare in Mainz (M 171).

[*Original extant, in the municipal library at Mainz (M 167).*] [R 19:11]

1455
Nov. 6

On 6 November, 1455, as enjoined by the Court at Mainz, Gutenberg's partner, Johann Fust, swears before a Notary and seven witnesses to the veracity of his statement previously made, that he had borrowed money on Gutenberg's behalf. The verdict contingent upon the swearing of this oath had already been pronounced at the hearing. The records are lost. But happily a brief review of the case was given before the oath-taking and recorded in the Notary's instrument.

Fust's loan, as stated in this review, had been made on two occasions, each in the sum of eight hundred *gulden*, the second having been made for their joint profit from "the work of the books" (M 185). Having borrowed *sechczendehalp hundert gulden*, having annually given rent, interest, and compound interest, and still owing part at the present time,

> . . . *do ich dan jerlichs gult, solt vnd schaden geben han vnd auch noch eins teils biss schuldig bin* . . .

Fust claims six *gulden* annually as interest on each hundred so borrowed, and asks also for interest on such borrowed money as had not been used for their common work—

> *Do rechen ich vor ein iglich hundert gulden, die ich also ussgenommen hain, wie obgeschrieben stet, jerlich sess gulden: was ym dez selben ussgenummen geldes worden ist, das nit uff vnser beder werck gangen ist, das sich in rechnung erfindet, do von heischen ich ym den soldt noch lude des spruche . . .*

Although Johann Fust reported both of his major loans of eight hundred *gulden* together with the accrued interest, the Court (according to the rather ambiguously worded verdict quoted in the Notary's instrument) apparently did not concern itself with financial affairs prior to Fust's entrance into partnership with Gutenberg at the time of the second loan—requiring the payment of interest on the eight hundred *gulden* advanced at that time, plus interest on whatever portion of that loan had not been used for their common work and on such money as Fust had borrowed to meet interest payments. The verdict reads:

> *Wan Johann Guttenberg sin rechnung gethain hat von allen innemen vnd ussgeben, dass er uff daz werck zu irer beider nocz ussgeben hait, was er dan men gelts dor uber enpfanngen vnd ingenummen hait, das sall in die achthundert gulden gerechent werdenn. Wer es aber, das sich an rechnung erfunde, das er ym me dan acht hundert gulden her uss geben hette, die nit in ieren gemeinen nocze kummen wern, sall er ym auch widder geben. Vnd brengt Johannes Fust by mit dem eyde oder redlicher kuntschafft, das er das obgeschreben gelt uff gulte ussgenummen vnd nit von sinem eigen gelde dar geluhen hat, so sall im Johann Gutenberg solch gulde auch ussrichten vnd beczalen nach lude dez zettels.*

We have no way of knowing whether these payments required by the Court threw Gutenberg into bankruptcy or whether he was able to salvage his type-casting tools, even if not his printing presses and types, or the "Gutenberg Bible" coming hot from the press.

This Helmasperger Instrument, as it is called from Ulrich Helmasperger, who notarized Fust's oath of veracity, has long been a matter of controversy. There is something about its phraseology that is tantalizingly intangible. To us its statements seem evasive. Linguistic points are involved in its translation, and the legal terminology of time and place. In short, interpretation of the instrument is not so simple as its rather archaic language would suggest.

(For a facsimile of the complete document, see p. 104 in RUPPEL, Aloys. *Johannes Gutenberg, sein Leben und sein Werk*, 1939, 1947. For an English rendering of the text, see p. 181–187 in McMURTRIE, D. C., ed. *The Gutenberg Documents*, 1941. For an analysis in German by an expert on medieval German law, see BLUM, Rudolf. *Der Prozess Fust gegen Gutenberg. Eine Interpretation des Helmaspergerschen Notariatsinstruments (Beiträge zum Buch- und Bibliothekswesen.* Bd. 2),Wiesbaden, 1954, although Dr. Blum rather confuses the issue by permitting himself to slip into the realm of conjecture. [For a review of Dr. Blum's monograph, see Dr. SCHOLDERER, p. 278–281 in *The Library*, 5th Ser., IX, 1954.] For further discussion of the lawsuit, see SCHMIDT-KUNSE-MÜLLER. *Rudolf Blums Interpretation des Prozesses Fust gegen Gutenberg* (p. 22–32 in *Gutenberg-Jahrbuch*, 1955); KOSCHOR-RECK, Walter. *Zum Prozess Fust gegen Gutenberg . . .* (p. 33–42 in *Gutenberg-Jahrbuch*, 1955); KANZOG, Klaus. *"Wiedergeben" und "Auch Wiedergeben" in Rechtsspruch des Helmaspergerschen Notariats-instruments zur Interpretation von Rudolf Blum* (p. 33–35 in *Gutenberg-Jahrbuch*, 1957.)

The dates of Fust's two loans are not known, although it has been computed on plausible grounds that the first loan may have been negotiated in mid-summer 1450, and the second possibly in 1452. From the large sums of money advanced to Gutenberg, it has long been believed that the loans may have had to do with the production of the "Gutenberg Bible," known to have been off the press at some time prior to August 1456.

Gutenberg, so it is stated in the Notary's instrument, had not been present at the swearing of the oath. Instead, he had sent Heinrich Gunther, sometime pastor of St. Christopher's at Mainz [*Gutenberg Jahrbuch*, 1956, p. 62–71] to report on what took place (M 182). He also sent his servant, Bechtolff von Hanau—possibly Berthold Ruppel, the printer who established the first press at Basel, about 1468—and Heinrich Keffer, who may have been the Heinrich Kefer who printed at Nuremberg in 1473, or possibly earlier. Of the seven men who witnessed the oath, four are entered as "Burghers of Mainz" and two as "Clerics of the city and diocese of Mainz" (M 187). Of the latter group, one is entered as Peter

Girnssheim, presumably the Peter Schoeffer of Gernsheim, a calligrapher, who became an employee of Johannes Fust and later a prominent printer in his own right.

[*The original Helmasperger Instrument, as this document is called, is in the library at the University of Gottingen.*] [R 19:13]

[In his paper on *Gutenberg and the B36 Group: A Re-consideration,* Mr. George D. Painter discusses the Helmasperger Instrument as a dissolution of partnership without ill will, as the result of which Gutenberg came off rather well.]

1457
June 21

According to a document dated 21 June, 1457, "Johann Gudenberg," layman of the diocese of Mainz, was one of five witnesses at the sale of certain parcels of real estate encumbered with the annual payment of thirty *malders* of wheat (M 190), to the Church of St. Victor Without the Walls, near Mainz. The document is significant because it is one of hardly more than half a dozen documents that indicate Gutenberg's whereabouts during the long years of his career. The document is also important in that it indicates his standing as an active and respected citizen and, therefore, his presumable solvency subsequent to the dissolution of his partnership with Fust.

[*Original extant, in the municipal library at Mainz* (M 188).] [R 20:1]

1458
Oct.

According to Dr. Karl Dziatzko, p. 47–49 in his *Beiträge zur Gutenbergsfrage (Sammlung Bibliothekswissenschaftlicher Arbeiten.* II. Berlin, 1889), three transcripts—located at the Bibliothèque Nationale, the Bibliothèque de l'Arsenal, and [with unimportant additions] at the Vatican Library—record that King Charles VII of France, having learned that Johann Gutenberg, a resident of Mainz, dextrous in the cutting and printing of type, had invented the art of printing, in October 1458 ordered the masters of the mint to send someone well qualified to learn the new art secretly and to bring it to France. The original record of the order is not known. The texts of the two transcripts located in Paris are quoted by Dziatzko. The one at the Bibliothèque Nationale, apparently written in 1559 in a codex [Fonds franc. 5524, fol. 152–153] recording the "Monnoyes de France" from 1179 to the reign of Henri II, was originally in the Bibliotheca Baluziana. Its text as quoted by Dziatzko is as follows:
Le IIIIme Jour doctobre mil IIIIcLVIII Ledz Sr roy ayant entendu que

Messre Jehan guthenberg chlr demourant a mayence pays dallemiagne home adextre en tailles et caracteres de poincons auoit mis en lumiere Linvention de imprimer par poincons et carracteres curieulx de tol tresor ledz Sr Roy auroit mande aux gñaulx de ses monnoyes [mint] Luy nommer psonnes biens entendues aladz taille et pour ennoyer audit Lieu secrettement soy informer deladz forme et manniere deladz invention, entendre concevoir et apprandre Lart dicelle A quoy feust sattisfaict audz Sr et par nicolas Jenson faust entreprins tant Ledz voyage que semblable-ment de parvenir a Lintelligence dudz art dimpression audz Royaulme de france. [Nicolaus Jenson, the engraver selected by the masters of the mint for this mission, is possibly the subsequent Venetian printer of that name. If so, this may account for the fine workmanship of Jenson's Venetian press. It has been suggested that the death of Charles VII is responsible for the fact that a press was not established in France at this early date. Another school of thought considers this reference to Jenson a myth.]

1461/62   According to accounts extant at St. Thomas Chapter in Strasbourg, after 1458 Gutenberg did not pay interest (M 195, 158) on the loan which he had received from the Chapter in 1442 (M 143). There-fore the Dean and Chapter of St. Thomas, on the Friday after Easter, 1461, addressed a petition to the Holy Roman Empire's imperial judge at Rottweil, praying for action (M 199). [*Original memorial lost; contemporary copy in archives of St. Thomas Chapter* (M 199).]

     The record of defaults of payment on the part of Gutenberg and his co-debtor, Martin Brechter, continues in the account-books of the Chapter until 1473/74, at which time the debt was written off (M 204). The record also includes the sums spent by the Chapter in the effort to collect the debt (M 205). Apparently the direful penalties of 12 January, 1441 [*q.v.*] were not imposed.

     [*Records extant, in the archives of St. Thomas Chapter* (M 201).] [R 20:6]

1465   In the course of a document dated at Eltville, 17 January, 1465,
Jan. 17   "We, Adolff . . . declare . . . that we have recognized the agreeable and voluntary services which our dear, faithful Johann Gudenberg has rendered . . . therefore, and by special dispensation, have ad-mitted and received him as our servant and courtier . . . Moreover, we . . . shall . . . each and every year . . . clothe him . . . like one of

our noblemen, and have . . . given to him . . . twenty *malder* of grain and two *fuder* of wine for the use of his household . . . and also exempt him graciously, as long as he lives, . . . and remains our servant, from watch duty, military service, taxation and sundries . . ." (M 201).

[*Original lost; early transcript at Würzburg* (M 216).] [R 20:7]

1467–
1468
In the 1467–1468 records in the *Liber fraternitatis* of the St. Victor Brotherhood, on leaf 7, verso, "Hengin Gudenberg, citizen of Mainz" is listed among the living lay brothers and sisters of the Brotherhood of the Church of St. Victor, Outside the Walls, of Mainz. On leaf 12, verso, his name again appears, among the deceased lay brothers and sisters.

[*Original codex extant, at Darmstadt.* (M 212)] [R 20:9]

1468
Feb. 26
In a promissory letter addressed to Adolf, Archbishop of Mainz, on 26 February, 1468, Dr. Conrad Humery states that in view of the fact that "my gracious and beloved lord . . . has graciously permitted *ettliche* forms, letters, instruments, and other things pertaining to the work of printing, which Johann Gutenberg has left after his death, and which have belonged and still belong to me, to come into my possession, therefore I, to honor and please his Grace, . . . do bind myself to use . . . said forms for printing" only within the city of Mainz . . . (M 219).

[*Original lost; early transcript at Wurzburg.*] [R 20:10]

[The date of Gutenberg's death is given as 3 February, 1468 in a manuscript note credibly assigned to Leonhard Mengoss of the cathedral chapter of Eltville, who died in January 1473 (Ruppel, A. *Gutenbergs Tod und Begräbnis*, 1968, p. 7–9; Abb. 4).]

The Gutenberg Tradition as stated in the Printed Books of the Fifteenth Century 1468–1499

Printed Tributes to
Gutenberg, 1468–1499

1468

JUSTINIANUS. Institutiones (with the *Glossa ordinaria* of Accursius). Mainz: Peter Schoeffer, 24 May, 1468. f°.

> *Fol. 103 verso; sig.* [N₆] *verso*: . . . He, Who is greater than Solomon, pleased to recognize men honored in art, brought forth these two men skilled in cutting letters—the two Johns of Mainz, distinguished first printers of books.
>
> And with them, to the pantheon they sought, came Peter—later in the race, but first to enter—made skillful in the art of engraving by Him Who alone bestows genius and light . . .
>
> *Ref*: GW 7580; BMC I 25; L-H 29; Stillw (G &C) 17; Goff J-506.
>
> *N.B*: Thus only a few months after Gutenberg's death, Peter Schoeffer paid tribute to his acknowledged predecessors and launched his advertising policy as a printer. Due to Fust's death and Schoeffer's marriage with his daughter, Schoeffer was now the head of the printing firm which, through advertising and his policy of out-of-town selling, became one of the leading houses in Europe during the remainder of the century.
>
> This tribute—to Johann Gutenberg, Johann Fust, and himself—Schoeffer repeated in his 1472 edition of Justinianus (Goff J-508). He used it again in his 1473 edition of the *Decretales* of Gregorius IX (Goff G-447). But in the latter, with a view to somewhat stronger publicity, Schoeffer inserted a caption, reading "The Type of the First Masters of the Art and a Panegyric to Peter."

1470/71

BARZIZIUS, Gasparinus. Orthographia. [Paris: Ulrich Gering, Martin Krantz & Michael Friburger, soon after 1 January, 1470/71.] 4°.

> *Fol. 1 verso—2 verso*: GUILLERMUS FICHETUS PARIENSIS ... ROBERTO GAGUINO ... SALUTEM: I speak with regard to the renaissance of humanistic

studies, to which, if I read the signs aright, the order of new book-makers has brought great light, whom Germany within our memory has poured forth everywhere, as did the Trojan horse of yore. For they say that not far from the city of Mainz, there was a certain Johann who bore the surname Gutenberg, who first of all men thought out the art of printing by which books are made, not written with a reed as former books were made, nor by pen as we make them, but by metal letters—and that indeed with speed, elegance and beauty. He was a man surely worthy of having all the muses, all the arts, and all the voices of those who delight in books honor him with divine praise, and prefer him to gods and goddesses, the more for the reason that he has vouchsafed a nearer and more present help to culture and its devotees ... Moreover, the illustrious Gutenberg invented far more divine and praiseworthy things, in so much as he cut letters of such a sort that whatever can be said, or thought, can immediately be written and copied and handed down to the memory of generations that are to come ...

Ref: GW 3691; Hain 2680; Stillw (G &C) 18.

N.B: A quotation from a printed letter written by Guillaume Fichet—a professor at the Sorbonne, who had been instrumental in the recent establishing of the first press in Paris—which gives a cultivated writer's understanding of the invention of printing and of its importance. The letter was addressed on 1 January, 1470/71 to his friend Roger Gaguin, 1432–1502, the leading French·humanist of the time. It is known only in the copy at Basel of the *Orthographia* (GW 3691), printed at Paris by Gering, Krantz and Friburger soon after it was written; and also as a separate (or imperfect copy of the *Orthographia*) said to be at Freiburg im Breisgau.

Fac: Facsimiles of the so-called Fichet Letter were issued under the editorship of L. Sieber, Basel, 1887; of Léopold Delisle, Paris, 1889; and of D. C. McMurtrie, New York, 1927.

1474

RICCOBALDUS FERRARIENSIS. Chronica summorum Pontificum Imperatorumque. Rome: Joannes Philippus de Lignamine, 14 July, 1474. 4°.

Fol. 121 recto-verso: JACOBUS CALLED GUTENBERG, NATIVE OF STRASBOURG, and another whose name was Fust, skilled in printing letters on parchment with metal forms were known, both of them, to be pulling three hundred sheets a day at Mainz, a city of Germany ...

Ref: H ★10857; BMC IV 33; Stillw (G &C) 19; Goff R-187.

N.B: A statement generally accepted as referring to the year 1458, since it occurs among the early entries under the pontificate of Pius II (1458–1464). Printed by the first press in Italy operated by a non-German. Its producer was a courtier who, as physician to Pope Sixtus IV, took up printing as a hobby and brought out some creditable books between 1470 and 1476, and again in a second period from 1481 to 1484.

1483

EUSEBIUS. Chronicon, *with the additions of Prosper, Matthaeus Palmerius and Matthias Palmerius* (Tr: Hieronymus. Ed: Johannes Lucilius Santritter). Venice: Erhard Ratdolt, 13 September, 1483. 4°.

> *Sig. u₃ verso*: IT IS BEYOND THE POWER OF WORDS to express how much students of letters owe to the Germans. For by Johann Gutenberg zum Jungen, knight of Mainz am Rhein, a man possessed of great genius, a method was discovered in 1440 for the printing of books. At the present time it is being diffused in nearly all parts of the earth . . .
>
> *Ref*: GW 9433; HC ★6717; BMC V 287; Stillw (G &C) 19; Goff E-117.
>
> *N.B*: This succinct statement regarding the beginning of the art of printing is of special interest because it was published little more than forty years after the date to which it relates. There must have been many persons alive, as presumably Santritter and Ratdolt, to whom the 1440s were within easy memory. The statement was not refuted and no counterclaims were made. It was on the strength of this statement and of its repetition by Ulrich Zel, as quoted in the *Cologne Chronicle* of 1499 [*see below*], together with such activities as are indicated in the early documentary sources, that the international celebration of the five-hundredth anniversary of the invention of printing was held in 1940.

JACOBUS PHILIPPUS DE BERGAMO. Supplementum chronicarum. Venice: Bernardinus Benalius, 23 August, 1483. f°.

> *Sig. CC₅ verso*: AT THIS TIME THE ART OF PRINTING BOOKS was discovered in Germany: some assert it was invented by Gutenberg, a Strasbourgian: others, by some one of another name—Fust. At all events, no art in the world could be more excellent, more praiseworthy, or more useful than this art of printing: and none more sacred or divine.
>
> *Ref*: HC ★2805; BMC V 370; IGI 5075; Stillw (G &C) 19; Goff J-208.
>
> *N.B*: Also issued by Boninus at Brescia, 1 December, 1485; and again by Benalius at Venice, 15 December, 1486 (Goff J-209, J-210). In the first two editions, the name of Nicolaus Jenson appears as a possible third candidate. In Benalius's second edition, 1486, however, and in later Venetian editions issued by Bernardinus Rizus (Goff J-211, J-212), the reference to Jenson is omitted. Although one of the most skillful and outstanding printers of the fifteenth century, Jenson was neither the inventor of printing nor the first printer of Venice—matters which were taken care of in no uncertain terms by Ulrich Zel as quoted in the *Cologne Chronicle* of 1499 [*see below*] and which are well substantiated by the records.

1492

BOSSIUS, Donatus. Chronica Bossiana. Milan: Antonius Zarotus, 1 March, 1492. f°.

Sig. r₈ verso: THE INVENTION OF PRINTING—In this year the art of printing books, helpful to all branches of learning, was invented by John Gutenberg, a German.

Ref: GW 4952; H *3667; BMC V 722; Stillw (G & C) 20; Goff B-1040.

N.B: Although more concerned with the ecclesiastical and local history of Milan than with history in general, the author paused to insert under 1457 this brief tribute to the value of Gutenberg's invention.

1499

DIE CRONICA VAN DER HILLIGER STAT VAN COELLEN. Cologne: Johann Koelhoff the Younger, 23 August, 1499. f°.

Fol. "312" recto: OF THE ART OF PRINTING: WHEN, WHERE, AND BY WHOM THE REMARKABLE ART OF PRINTING BOOKS WAS IN-VENTED . . . This highly worthy art was first invented in Germany, at Mainz, on the Rhine. And to the German people it is a great honour that such ingenious men are to be found among them. It came to pass in the year of our Lord, anno Domini 1440, and from that time until one wrote [14]50, this art and all that relates to it was experimented with. And in the year of our Lord when one wrote 1450—that was a golden year—printing began. And the first book to be printed was the Bible in Latin, with type as large as the type nowadays used in the printing of Missals.

However, although the art was first invented in Mainz in the manner in which it has been generally practised from that time to this, the first stages of the develop-ment are found in Holland in the Donatuses, which were printed before this time. From and out of these is derived the beginning of the Foremost Art, which is now much more skillfully and more cleverly invented than that earlier manner was, and which has been practised more and more dextrously with the passing of the years.

Moreover, a certain Omnebonus writes in his preface to the book called Quintilianus, and also in some other books, that a Walloon from France, named Nicolaus Jenson, was the very first to invent this masterly art—but that obviously is not true. For, there are men still living who can testify that books were being printed in Venice before Nicolaus Jenson first came to the point where he began to cut and make ready his type.

On the contrary, the first inventor of printing was a citizen of Mainz, and he was born in Strasbourg and called Squire Johann Gutenberg. Moreover, from Mainz the Foremost Art came first to Cologne, thereafter to Strasbourg, and thereafter to Venice. The beginning and progress of the Foremost Art was told me by that honourable man Ulrich Zell of Hanau, a printer in Cologne even now, anno 1499, through whom the art first came to Cologne . . .

Ref: GW 6688; HC *4989; BMC I 299; Stillw (G & C) 21–22; Goff C-476.

N.B: This account of the invention of printing in the *Cologne Chronicle*, as it is called, provoked much controversy a century ago. Either Ulrich Zel, who had introduced printing into Cologne about 1465, or the editor of the *Chronicle* to whom he made this report, managed to misstate Gutenberg's place of birth and to confuse the priority of Strasbourg over that of Cologne in the spread of printing. These errors caused German scholars to discredit other statements, particularly of course that relating to Holland. Dutch scholars, on the other hand, seized upon the statement regarding the presence of *Donatuses* in Holland as proof that printing was invented there. Out of this hypothesis—supported by folklore as set forth in Hadrian de Jonghe's *Batavia*, 1588—there grew the fiery Dutch and German controversy over the invention of printing, which began nearly a century ago and raged intermittently for decades.

Ulrich Zel had been correct in his statement that printing had been established at Venice before the time of Nicolaus Jenson. Printing had been introduced in Venice by Johann von Speyer, who produced two editions of Cicero and a Pliny in 1469. And the official Privilege, which had been granted him for a five-year period and which was in force when he suddenly died in the early part of 1470, had precluded the establishing of any other Venetian press up to that time. Consequently Jenson, whose first book is dated 1470, cannot have set up his press until after the first printer's death.

Mon: For a note discussing the inaccuracies in Zel's account, see C. F. BÜHLER, p. 374 in the BIBLIOGRAPHICAL SOCIETY of AMERICA. *Papers. 50, 1956.*

MARSILIUS de INGHEN. Oratio continens dictiones clausulas et elegantias oratorias. [Mainz: Peter von Friedberg, after 10 July, 1499.] 4°.

Fol. 22 recto: TO THE INVENTOR OF THE ART OF PRINTING, BLESSED IN MEMORY, SACRED TO GOD, THE GREATEST AND BEST—TO JOHANN GENSFLEISCH, ORIGINATOR OF THE PRINTING ART, deserving of highest praise from every nation and tongue, Adam Gelthus has placed this inscription to the memory of his name, whose bones rest in peace in the Church of St. Francis at Mainz.

EPIGRAM OF JACOB WIMPHELING OF SLETSTADT UPON THE SAME INVENTOR—

O blessed Gensfleisch, through thee
is Germany blessed and praised
throughout the earth.
Thou, O Johann, in the city of Mainz,
strengthened by talent divine,
art the first to stamp letters in bronze.
Much do religion, the wisdom of the Greeks,
and the Latin tongue owe to thee.

Ref: HC *10781; BMC I 49; Stillw (G &C) 20; Goff M-282.
N.B: The memorial inscribed by Adam Gelthuss, who was presumably a kinsman of Gutenberg, as included in this early collection of quotations, is discussed by Dr. Ruppel in a chapter on the death and burial place of Gutenberg.

Gutenberg—Tributes, 1499 (continued)

    Mon: RUPPEL, Aloys. *Johannes Gutenberg, sein Leben and sein Werk.* Berlin, 1939, p. 80–89; 1947, p. 68–75; *Der Totenschild am Grabe Gutenbergs* (p. 35–42 in *Gutenberg-Jahrbuch* 1937). [For an account of Wimpheling, 1450–1528, see SCHOLDERER, V. *Jacob Wimpheling, an early Strassburg humanist*, p. 69–96 in BIBLIOGRAPHICAL SOCIETY. *Transactions.* 13, 1913–1915.]

Appendix B

Undated Imprints assigned to
The Netherlands

Appendix B
Type groups and Eponymous Presses

ABECEDARIUM sue Pater noster:
    Abecedarium, 100 G. type (*Hellinga type 8*)—B:1.
    Donatus, 120 G. type (*Hellinga type 7*)—B:6d.
AESOPUS [Lorenzo Valla, *tr.*] 113 G. type (*Hellinga "Valla" type 3*)—B:2.
    Petrarca—B:8.
DONATUS, 122 G. type (*Hellinga type 6*)—B:6e.
PONTANO, 142/144 type (*Hellinga type 4*)—B:12.
    Donatus—B:6a.
    Porphyrius—B:13.
SALICETO, 123/124 G. type (*Hellinga type 5*)—B:15.
    Alexander de Villa Dei, *Doctrinale*—B:3a.
    Cato—B:4.
    Donatus—B:6b.
    Pindarus Thebanus—B:9.
    Pius II, *Pont. Max.*—B:10, B:11.
    Torquemada—B:17.
SPECULUM HUMANAE SALVATIONIS, 100/111 G. type (*Hellinga types 1, 2*)—B:16.
    Alexander de Villa Dei, *Doctrinale*—B:3b.
    Cato—B:5.
    Donatus—B:6c.
    Manuale—B:7.
    Psalmi poenitentiales—B:14.

    Donatus, transitional 98/103 G. type (*Hellinga type 2★*)—B:6c.

A century ago these titles were assigned provisionally by Henry Bradshaw to the *Printer of the Speculum*, and the assignment has become traditional. In reality, however, eight fonts of type and several variants were employed in their production. Apart from the infrequent use of four of these fonts (Hellinga nos. 3, 6, 7, 8), as known through fragments extant today, all of the other imprints are in the types of the Pontano, the Saliceto, or the *Speculum*, thus possibly indicating the existence of several presses.

    The traditional assignment of the group to the *Printer of the Speculum*, however, has served an important function in keeping these unidentified pieces together and apart from all others. As a convenience it serves a purpose and it serves it well, provided it is recognized as such. In volume IX of the British Museum's *Catalogue of books printed in the XVth century*, as a matter of evolution, the assignment has been altered to *Printer of the text of the Speculum*; cognizance is taken of the fact that the typographical printing of the text and the impressing of the woodcut illustrations by friction were presumably not done at the same establishment; and it is conceded (BMC IX, p. 1) that the use of the woodcuts by Johann Veldener at Utrecht in 1481—which had caused Bradshaw to assign the *Speculum* to Utrecht—"may from the first have been the property of another owner."

    In view of the typographical questions involved and also the disparity in the texts chosen for printing, noted above in the Preface to the present volume, it would seem that the assigning of these pieces to three or four or more eponymous presses, as indicated above, may serve to carry the matter a step further in the effort to identify these seemingly unidentifiable imprints.

APPENDIX B

Undated Imprints assigned to
The Netherlands

[*For discussion of the various types employed in the so-called Costeriana as noted below, see* L. A. SHEPPARD (BMS IX xxi–xxiv 1); *and the marginal note in* BMC Reprint IX, p. xxi. *See also* W. *and* L. HELLINGA I, p. 4–9, *where the groups are discussed under the term Prototypography. The intermingled use of Hellinga types 2–5 in various items would seem to indicate that these types (and possibly Hellinga type 1) belonged to one press. In view of the assignment of the first Latin edition of the Speculum (B: 16a, below) to [c. 1468]—in Stevenson-Briquet, vol. 1, p. *95—it is possible that other items in 110/111 G. (Hellinga type 1) may have been printed before 1470.*]

ABECEDARIUM sive Pater Noster.

B:1   ——— [The Netherlands: in 100 G. type (Hellinga type 8), n.d.]

    Ref: Camp 1; Hellinga I 9, II 457.
    Cop: Municipal Library, Haarlem.
    N.B: A primer for early instruction in piety as well as in reading. A small octavo of four leaves. In type that is smaller but similar to that of a 27-line Donatus (B:6d) known in a fragment at Uden.
    Fac: HOLTROP, J. W. *Monuments typographiques des Pays-Bas au quinzieme siècle*, 1868, no. 12.

AESOPUS.

B:2   Fabulae (Tr: Lorenzo Valla, *d.* 1457). [The Netherlands (Utrecht?): in 113 G. type (Hellinga Valla-type 3), *c.* 1472 or earlier.]

    Add: PETRARCA, Francesco, *d.* 1374. De salibus virorum illustrium ac Facetiis.
    Ref: GW 315; BMC IX 3; Camp 30; Hellinga I 5.
    Cop: London, Cambridge, The Hague, Bruxelles, Mainz, Berlin.
    Fac: Hellinga II, pl. 7 and 8.

ALEXANDER de Villa Dei (Alexandre de Villedieu; *called* Alexander Gallus), *fl.*, 1170–1230.

B:3   Doctrinale. [The Netherlands (Utrecht?): *c.* 1472 or earlier.]

Alexander (continued)

a) SALICETO TYPE:

28-line edition, in 123/124 G. type; known in 3 fragments:

> *Ref*: Kron 108a:1; GW 933 (both of which assign the date [before 1470?]); Hellinga II 459.
> *Cop*: The Hague, Ghent, Oxford.

29-line edition, in 123/124 G. type; known in 27 fragments and a variant:

> *Ref*: Kron 108b–d; GW 934, 935 *var*; BMC IX 5; Hellinga II 459; Bühler V; Stillwell A374; Goff A-413.
> *Cop*: The Hague, London, Cambridge (2, 1 *var*), and elsewhere.—New York (PML).

b) SPECULUM TYPE:

32-line edition, in 110/111 G. type; known in 26 fragments:

> *Ref*: Kron 108e–f; GW 936; BMC IX 3; Hellinga II 458; Bühler I–IV; Stillwell A375–A379; Goff A-414—A-419.
> *Cop*: The Hague, London, and elsewhere.—Camarillo (ELDL); New York (CHP; PML, 3); San Marino (HEHL).
> *Mon*: BÜHLER, C. F. *New Coster fragments of the Doctrinale* (*Gutenberg-Jahrbuch*, 1938); *A Note on Zedler's Coster theory* (B.S.A. *Papers*, 37, 1943). ZEDLER, G. *Der älteste Buchdruck und das frühhöllandische Doktrinale des Alexander de Villa Dei*, Leiden, 1936. TRONNIER, A. *Ein "Costerfund"* ... (*Gutenberg-Jahrbuch*, 1926). REICHLING, D. *Das Doctrinale des Alexander de Villa-Dei* (*Monumenta Germaniae Paedagogica*, XII, 1893).

CATO (*also called* Dionysius Cato *or* Disticha Catonis).

B:4 —— [The Netherlands (Utrecht?): in 123/124 G. (*Saliceto*) type, about 1470.]

21-line edition:

> *Ref*: GW 6250; Kron 405a; Hellinga II 459; Stillwell C258; Goff C-288.
> *Cop*: Pierpont Morgan Library, New York (2 ff, *vell*).

B:5 —— [The Netherlands (Utrecht?): in 110/111 G. (*Speculum*) type, about 1472.]

21-line edition:

> *Ref*: GW 6251; HC 4707; Camp 405; Hellinga II 458.
> *Cop*: John Rylands Library, Manchester.

26-line edition:

> *Ref*: GW 6252; Pell 3406.
> *Cop*: Bibliothèque Nationale, Paris.

DONATUS, Aelius, *a fourth-century grammarian, the teacher of St. Jerome.*

B:6   Ars minor. [The Netherlands (Utrecht?): *c.* 1472 or earlier.]

a) PONTANO TYPE:

24-line edition, in 142/144 G. (Hellinga no. 4) type; known in 18 fragments showing at least 7 variant type-settings:

> *Ref*: Kron 633:1-10; GW 8723-8738; Hellinga I 16, II 457; Goff D-319.
> *Cop*: The Hague, Paris, and elsewhere.—Boston (BPubL) (1 fol., vell).

b) SALICETO TYPE:

26-line edition, in 123/124 G. (Hellinga no. 5) type; known in 5 fragments showing at least 2 variant type-settings:

> *Ref*: Kron 633:11-13; GW 8739-8742.
> *Cop*: The Hague, Heidelberg, Dusseldorf, Darmstadt, Cologne.

27-line edition, in 123/124 G. (Hellinga no. 5) type; known in 41 fragments showing at least 15 variant type-settings:

> *Ref*: Kron 633:14-41: Kron (More) p. 134; GW 8743-8780; Stillwell D265-D267; Goff D-321—D-326.
> *Cop*: The Hague, Mainz, and elsewhere.—Bloomington (InUL); Boston (BPubL); Chicago (NewL); New York (PML, 2); Mr. Paul Mellon, Upperville, Va. (See also *Gutenberg Jahrbuch*, 1959, p. 58).

c) SPECULUM TYPE:

27-line edition, in 110/111 G. (Hellinga no. 1) type; known in 1 fragment only:

> *Ref*: Kron 633:42; GW 8781.
> *Cop*: University Library, Louvain.

28-line edition, in 98/103 (Hellinga no. 2*) type; known in 1 fragment only.

> *Ref*: Kron 633a; Hellinga I 5, II 457.
> *Cop*: Ruusbroecgenootschap, Antwerp.
> *Fac*: Hellinga II, pl. 4, 5.

28-line edition, in 110/111 G. (Hellinga no. 1) type; known in 9 fragments showing 5 variant type-settings:

Donatus, B:6c (continued)

    Ref: Kron 633:43-48; GW 8782-8789.
    Cop: Leiden, Haarlem, The Hague, and elsewhere.

30-line edition, in 110/111 G. (Hellinga no. 1) type; known in 19 fragments showing at least 7 variant type-settings, including that of a French version:

    Ref: Kron 633:49-64; BMC IX 3; GW 8790-8806; Goff D-327.
    Cop: The Hague, London, and elsewhere.—Bloomington (InUL).
    N.B: A French version, at Utrecht, is cited in Camp (3rd Supp) 615a. Entered in Kronenberg as "Des viij parties doraison. (Utrecht? Dutch Prototypography). 4°."
    Fac: Zedler, Von Coster zu Gutenberg, Taf. XV.
    Mon: SHEPPARD, L. A. *The Speculum Printer's editions of Donatus, a numerical estimate* (p. 63-65 in *Gutenberg-Jahrbuch*, 1954).

d) ABECEDARIUM TYPE:

27-line edition in 120 G. (Hellinga no. 7) type; known in 1 fragment only.

    Ref: GW 8807; Hellinga I 9, II 457.
    Cop: Uden.
    N.B: Cited in Hellinga as similar to Abecedarium type 100 G. (B:1, above).
    Fac: Hellinga II, pl. 13.

31-line edition, in 100 G., small Abecedarium (Hellinga no. 8) type; known in 1 fragment only.

    Ref: GW 8815; Hellinga I 9, II 457.
    Cop: The Hague.
    Fac: Hellinga II, pl. 14.

e) UNASSIGNABLE TYPE:

26-line edition, in 122 G. (Hellinga no. 6) type; known in 2 fragments.

    Ref: Kron 633:66; GW 8808-8809; Stillwell D264; Goff D-320.
    Cop: Cologne.—Scheide Collection [*on deposit at Princeton Un.*].

27-line edition, in 119/122 G. (Hellinga no. 6?) type; known in 4 fragments.

    Ref: Kron 633:67; BMC IX 109; GW 8810-8813.
    Cop: Haarlem, The Hague, London, Dusseldorf.
    Fac: Hellinga II, pl. 12 (GW 8812), *ante 1480*.

HOMER. [For an abridgement of the Iliad, *see* B:9.]

MANUALE.

B:7 —— [The Netherlands (Utrecht?): in 110/111 G. (*Speculum*; *Hellinga type* 1), n.d.]

> *Ref*: Camp 1174; Polain 2503; Hellinga I p. 4.
> *Cop*: Royale Bibliothèque, Bruxelles, *fragment*.
> *N.B*: A manual for altar-servers. *Text begins*: Omnipotens deus et dimissis omnibus peccatis vestris perducat nos . . .

PETRARCA, Francesco, *d.* 1374.

B:8 De salibus virorum illustrium ac Facetiis. (*Issued with* AESOPUS. Fabulae. *See* B:2.)

> *N.B*: According to BMC IX 4, the text consists of extracts from Book II of Petrarch's *Res memoranda*. The *Facetiae* have been identified as extracts from Poggius Florentinus.

PINDARUS THEBANUS, *attributed*.

B:9 Iliados epitome, de graeco in latinum versa. (*Issued with* Saliceto. *See* B:15.)

> *Ref*: Oates 3295 (Camp 1416 *note*); Hellinga II 459.
> *N.B*: Possibly issued also in separate form (Camp 1416, 1417). Although the attribution to Pindar, *fl.* 522–442 B.C., is now questioned, it was through this abridgement that Homer was known for centuries. Its author may possibly be identifiable with Silius Italicus of the first century A.D., since two acrostics within the text spell out the name Italicus.
> *Fac*: Hellinga II, pl. 11.

PIUS II, *Pontifex Maximus* (Eneas Sylvio Piccolomini), *d.* 1464.

B:10 Contra luxuriosos et lasciuos tractatus de amore. Pro laude Homeri. (*Issued with* Saliceto. *See* B:15.)

B:11 De mulieribus prauis [*i.e.,* Contra luxriosos . . . tractatus . . ., *as in* B:10]. De laude atque epitaphiis virorum illustrium tractatus. (*Issued with* Pontano, but in 123 G. (*Saliceto*) type. *See* B:12.)

> *N.B*: The authenticity of the second tract has been questioned. For discussion of the relation of these texts to those of Pius II in the Saliceto, see BMC IX 4: Pontano.

PONTANO, Ludovico (Ludovicus Pontanus; *called* Ludovico de Roma), 1409–1439.

B:12 Singularia in causis criminalibus. [The Netherlands (Utrecht?): in 142/144 G. (*Pontano*; *Hellinga no. 4*) type, not before 1458, not after 1472?]

> *Add*: Pius II, *Pont. Max.*, *d.* 1464. De mulieribus prauis. De laude ... virorum illustrium tractatus (in 123 G. (*Saliceto*) type).
>
> *Ref*: Camp 1186; BMC IX 4; Oates 3294; Hellinga I 6, II 457, 459; Stillwell P845; Goff P-926.
>
> *Cop*: The Hague, London, Cambridge—New York (PML); Providence (AmBM).
>
> *N.B*: The fact that the author is referred to as Eneas Silvius *poeta senensis* on fol. 40a, and as Pius II on fol. 45b, would indicate that this edition was printed after his elevation to the Papacy in 1458. The terminal date, 1472, is derived from a rubricator's in the Darmstadt copy of Saliceto (B:15) with which the latter portion of this volume, from fol. 45b onward, is typographically related.
>
> *Fac*: Hellinga II, pl. 9, 10.

PORPHYRIOS (Porphyrius), 233–*c.* 304.

B:13 Liber quinque praedicabilium. [The Netherlands (Utrecht?): in 142 G. (*Pontano*; *Hellinga no. 4*) type, n.d.]

> *Ref*: Kron 1437a; BMC IX xxii, *note*; Hellinga II 458.
>
> *Cop*: University of Utrecht, *1 leaf*.
>
> *N.B*: A fragment found in a binding made for the Augustinian Canons of Utrecht.

PSALMI POENITENTIALES.

B:14 —— [*Dutch.*] [The Netherlands (Utrecht?): in 110/111 G. (*Speculum*; *Hellinga no. 1*) type, n.d.]

> *Ref*: Camp 1459; Polain 3266, *fac*; Hellinga I 4.
>
> *Cop*: Bibliothèque Royale, Bruxelles, *fragment*.

SALICETO (Guglielmo Saliceti, of Piacenza; *called* Guilielmus de Saliceto), 1210–1277.

B:15 De salute corporis. [The Netherlands (Utrecht?): in 123 G. (*Saliceto*; *Hellinga no. 5*) type, not before 1458, not after 1472.]

> *Add*: TORQUEMADA, Juan de, *d.* 1468. De salute animae. PIUS II, *Pont. Max.*, *d.* 1464. Contra luxuriosos et lascius tractatus de amore.

Pro laude Homeri. PINDARUS Thebanus. Iliados epitome, de graeco in latinum versa.

Ref: Camp 1493 (+ 3rd Supp); BMC IX 1, 4; Polain 1837; Hellinga I 6, 7, II 457, 459; Stillw (AIS) 510.

Cop: The Hague, London, Bruxelles, Darmstadt (*var*).

N.B: A tract on hygiene. One of the earliest printed pieces of medical interest, the others being a medico-astrological calendar for 1457, an almanac for 1462, a medical section in the encyclopedia of Rabanus Maurus printed in 1467, and tracts by Jean Charlier de Gerson assigned to 1467. Not issued before the elevation of Eneas Sylvio Piccolomini to the Papacy in 1458, and probably not until after his death in 1464. The Darmstadt copy bears the rubricator's date 1472.

Fac: Hellinga II, pl. 11.

SPECULUM HUMANAE SALVATIONIS.

B:16 —— [The Netherlands (Utrecht?): in 110/111 G. (*Speculum*; *Hellinga no. 1*) type, *c.* 1470/71.]

N.B: The sequence of the four editions cited below is based on the state of the woodcut illustrations, as derived from Ottley and BMC II 2:

a) First Latin edition, in 110/111 G. (*Hellinga no. 1*) type.

  Ref: Camp 1570; H 14923; Hellinga I 4, II 457; Stillwell S586; Goff S-656.

  Cop: The Hague; Munich, with stamped or written date 1471; and elsewhere —Boston (MFArt); New York (NYPL).

  N.B: Stevenson-Briquet, p. *95, [*c.* 1468].

  Fac: Hellinga II, pl. 1.

b) First Dutch edition, in 100/111 G. (*Hellinga no. 12*) type, with a sheet in 103 G. (*Hellinga no. 2*) type.

  Ref: Camp 1571; BMC IX 2; Hellinga I 4, II 457, 458.

  N.B: Stevenson-Briquet, p. *95, [*c.* 1471].

  Cop: London.

  Fac: Hellinga II, pl. 3–5.

c) Second Latin edition, in 110/111 G. (*Hellinga no. 1*) type, with the text on 20 leaves produced by wood-engraving.

  Ref: Camp 1569; H 14922; BMC IX 2; Hellinga I 4; LC(LJRCat) 378; Stillwell S585; Goff S-657.

  Cop: The Hague, London, Berlin, and elsewhere—New York (PML); Washington (LC—Rosenwald Coll.).

  N.B: Stevenson-Briquet, p. *95, [*c.* 1474].

  Fac: Hellinga II, pl. 2.

d) Second Dutch edition, in 110/111 G. (*Hellinga no. 1*) type.

> *Ref*: Camp 1572; H 14924; Hellinga I 4; Stillwell S588; Goff S-659.
> *Cop*: Haarlem, Manchester(?), and elsewhere—San Marino (HEHL).
> *N.B*: Stevenson-Briquet, p. *95, [*c.* 1479].

TORQUEMADA, Juan de (called Turrecremata), *d.* 1468.

B:17   De salute animae. (Issued with SALICETO. *See no.* B:15.)

In addition to the titles listed above, fragments from two unidentified legal texts, in 142 G. (Pontano) type, are recorded as at the University of Utrecht. Also two other titles sometimes listed among these Dutch prototypographs have defied current identification—the so-called *Facetiae* of Lorenzo Valla and a *Tractatus* of Pius II. It is possible, however, that the latter reference may inadvertently apply to one of two works by Pius II (B:10 or B:11), since in each instance the word *Tractatus* occurs in the title. As for the *Facetiae* of Lorenzo Valla, the reference may be derived from Valla's translation of Aesop (B:2), the *incipit* of which begins with the words: *Facecie morales laurentij vallensis al's esopus grecus per dictum laurentiū translatus incipiunt feliciter.* There is also the possibility that it is a confused reference to the *Facetiae*, the extracts from the work of this title by Poggius Florentinus which Hellinga identifies in the additions to the Aesop (B:2, above), a work which includes Valla's Aesop in the Paris edition assigned to about 1474/75 (Goff P-857).

Index

Index

Includes authors and anonymous titles as cited in the main entries, variant author-forms, and cross-references. In instances where a work was issued with other titles, the entry-number is followed by that of the compilation, in parentheses. For subject and typographical analyses, for authors by periods and lists of commentators, editors, and translators, see the SUPPLEMENTARY SECTION, above. For reference-numbers which are enclosed in square brackets, see SUPPLEMENTARY SECTION E: Undated Imprints currently unassigned, or re-assigned to 1470 or later.

Abecedarium. See Appendix B, *no. 1.*

Accorso, Francesco (Accursius), *no. 121(140).*

Ackermann von Böhmen, nos. 29, 61.

Adolf II von Nassau, *no. 50. See also nos. 41n–44n.*

Aesopus. *See* Appendix B, *no. 2.*

Albinus Platonicus, *no. 149(150).*

Alcinous. *See* Albinus Platonicus.

Alexander de Villa Dei. *See* Appendix B, *no. 3.*

Alexandre de Villedieu. *See* Alexander de Villa Dei.

Almanach für Wein, no. 36.

Alonso de Borja. *See* Calixtus III, *Pont. Max.*

Alphabetum divini amoris, no. 80.

Andreae, Joannes, *jurist, no. 70(71).*

Antonino, *St., no. 122.*

Antoninus Florentinus. *See* Antonino, *St.*

Apuleius Madaurensis, Lucius, *no. 150.*

Aristeas, *no. 123(137).*

Aristotle:
   Ethica ad Nicomachum, no. 151.
   Oeconomica, no. 152(151).
   Politica, no. 153(151).

Ars minor. See Donatus, Aelius.

Astesanus de Ast, *O.F.M., nos. 154, 155.*

Augustinus, Aurelius, *St.*:
   De arte praedicandi, nos. 81, 82, 124.
   De civitate dei, nos. 96, 125, 126.
   De doctrina christiana, lib. IV. See De arte praedicandi.
   De ebrietate, no. 97(100).
   Enchiridion de fide, spe et caritate, no. 98.
   Expositio super symbolum, no. 99(100).
   Sermo super orationem dominicam, no. 100.
   De singularitate clericum, no. 101(102).
   De vita christiana, nos. 37, 102.

Aurbach, Johannes de, *theologian, no. 156.*

Balbi, Giovanni, (Balbus), *nos. 30, 157.*

Beichtbuechlein, no. 158.

Belial. *See no. 63.*

Benedictus XII, *Pont. Max., nos. 31(32), 103(107).*

Bernardus Silvester, *no. 159.*

Bertrandi del Goth. *See* Clemens V, *Pont. Max.*

Bessarion, *Patriarch, no. 160.*

Bible [*German*]: 60 lines, *no. 162.* —— 61 lines, *no. 84.*

Bible [*Latin*]: 36 lines, *no. 25.* —— 40 lines, *no. 21.* —— 41 lines, *no. 161; see also no. 135.* —— 42 *lines, no. 1.* —— 45 lines, *nos. 83, 127.* —— 47 lines, *no. 128.* —— 48 lines, 1462, *no. 51.* —— 49 lines, *no. 38.*

Biblia pauperum [German]: *nos. 52, 62.*

Biblia pauperum [Latin]: *no. 53.*

Bonaventura, *St.*, *nos. 85, 129.*

Boner, Ulrich, *nos. 39, 54.*

Bonifacius VIII, *Pont. Max.*, *nos. 32n, 71.*

Borja, Alonso de. *See* Calixtus III, *Pont. Max.*

Brunner, Johann, *nos. 86, 130.*

Caesar, Caius Julius, *no. 163.*

"Calendar for 1448." *See* Planet-table.

Calendar for 1457, *no. 13.*

Calixtus III, *Pont. Max.*, *nos. 14, 15.*

Canon missae, *no. 22.*

Catholicon. See Balbi, Giovanni.

Cato. *See* Appendix B, *nos. 4, 5.*

Chappe, Paulinus, *commissary*, *nos. 8n, 9n, 10n, 11n.*

Charlier de Gerson, Jean. *See* Gerson.

"Christian Cicero," The. *See* Lactantius Firmianus, Caelius.

Chrysostomus. *See* Joannes Chrysostomus.

Cicero, Marcus Tullius:

De amicitia, *nos. 164, 165(175), 166(174), 167(176).*

Brutus, *nos. 168, 169(179).*

Cato maior de senectute. *See* De amicitia.

De claribus oratoribus. *See* Brutus.

Epistolae ad familiaris, *nos. 104, 170, 171, 172.*

Laelius de amicitia. *See* De amicitia.

De officiis, *nos. 72, 73, 87, 173, 174, 175, 176.*

De optimo genere dicendi. *See* Orator.

Orator, *nos. 177(168), 178(179).*

De oratore, *nos. 74, 131, 132a, 179.*

Paradoxa stoicorum, *nos. 75(73), 88(87), 105, 180, 181(175), 182(174), 183(176).*

De senectute, *nos. 106, 184, 185(175), 186(174), 187(176).*

Somnium Scipionis, *nos. 188(184), 189(176).*

Tusculanae disputationes, *no. 190.*

Cisioianus [German], *no. 16.*

Clemens V, *Pont. Max.*:

Bulla: Exivi de paradiso, *nos. 33 (32), 107.*

Constitutiones, *nos. 32, 107.*

Clementine laws, *no. 32n.*

Columna, Guido de. *See* Supplementary Section E: Undated Imprints re-assigned to 1470 or later, *no.* [*132b*].

Congregationis Bursfeldensis observantia per Germaniam. *See* Psalterium Benedictinum.

Corpus juris civilis, *no. 140n.*

D'Andrea, Giovanni. *See* Andreae, Joannes, *jurist.*

D'Andrea de 'Bossi, Giovanni. *See* Supplementary Section: Editors.

Diether von Isenberg, *nos. 55, 56. See also nos. 40, 46, 50.*

Dionysius Cato. *See* Cato.

Disticha Catonis. *See* Cato.

Diurnale moguntinum, *no. 191.*

Donatus, Aelius, *nos. 3, 4, 23a-d, 76, 133, 134. See also* Appendix B, *no. 6.*

Duèse, Jacques. *See* Joannes XXII, *Pont. Max.*

Durand, Guillaume (Durandus; Duranti), *no. 26,* [*67*].

Eggestein, Heinrich, *no. 135.*

Expositio super canonem missae, *no. 192.*

Eyn manung der Cristenheit widder die Durken, no. 5.

Fons, Joannes. *See* Brunner, Johann.

Forma absolutionis, *no. 112.*

Formula for women, *no. 58.*

Fournier, Jacques. *See* Benedictus XII, *Pont. Max.*

Francis, *St.*, Rule of, *nos. 33 (32), 107.*

Friedrich III, *Emperor*, *no. 40.*

Gaetano, Benedetto. *See* Bonifacius VIII, *Pont. Max.*

Gellius, Aulus, *no. 193.*

Georgius Trapezuntius [George of Trepizond], *no. 92n.*

Gerson, Joannes:

Alphabetum divini amoris(?), *no. 80n.*

De arte moriendi, *no. 110.*

De cognitione castitatis, *no. 108a(112).*

Conclusiones de diversis materiis moralibus, no. 108b.

De confessione, *no. 110.*

De custodia linguae, *no. 194.*

Forma absolutionis sacramentalis, *no. 89(90).*

De modo vivendi omnium fidelium, no. 109(111).

Opus tripartitum, *no. 110.*

De passionibus animae, *no. 111.*

De pollutione nocturna, *nos. 90, 112.*

De pollutionibus diurnis, *no. 108a(112).*

Index

De praeceptis decalogi, no. 110.

Golden-tongued, The, *so called. See* Joannes Chrysostomus.

Goth, Bertrand de. *See* Clemens V, *Pont. Max.*

Greek characters. *See no. 78n.*

Gregorius I, *Pont. Max., St., no. 195.*

"Gutenberg Bible," *no. 1.*

Gutenberg documents, Analysis of the. *See* Appendix A., p. 74.

Hermes Trismegistos (Trismegistus), *no. 196(150).*

Hieronymus, *St., nos. 136, 137, 197.*

Homer. *See* Appendix B, *no. ix.*

Horatius Flaccus, Quintus, *nos. 77(73), 91(87).*

Hrabanus. *See* Rabanus Maurus.

Innocentius III, *Pont. Max., no. 138.*

Invention of printing. *See* Printing, Invention of.

Isidore of Sevilla, *no. 115n.*

Jacobus de Theramo, *no. 63.*

Jacques d'Euse. *See* Joannes XXII, *Pont. Max.*

Jerome, *St. See* Hieronymus, *St.*

Joannes XXII, *Pont. Max., nos. 34(32), 113(107).*

Joannes Andreae. *See* Supplementary Section: Editors.

Joannes Chrysostomus:

De eo quod nemo laeditur . . ., no. 198.

Homiliae super Matthaeum, no. 92.

De reparatione lapsi, no. 199.

Sermo de poenitentia, no. 139a(122).

Sermo super psalmum L: Miserere, nos. 93, 139b.

Sermones de patientia in Job, no. 114.

Joannes de Turrecremata. *See* Torquemada.

Johannes de Auerbach, *jurist. See no. 156n.*

Johannes von Saaz, *nos. 29n, 61n.*

Juan de Torquemada. *See* Torquemada.

Justinianus, Flavius Anicius, *Emperor, no. 140.*

Justinus, Marcus Junianus, *no. 201.*

Koppischt, Johann, von Aurbach. *See* Aurbach, Johannes de, *theologian.*

Lactantius Firmianus, Caelius, *nos. 78, 141.*

Levi, Solomon. *See* Pablo de Santa Maria.

Livius, Titus, *nos. 202, 203.*

Lothario de 'Conti (Lotharius). *See* Innocentius III, *Pont. Max.*

Lotharius, Printer of. *See no. 138.*

Lucanus, Marcus Annaeus, *no. 204.*

Ludovico de Roma. *See* Pontano, Ludovico.

Manuale. See Appendix B, *no. 7.*

Manung. See "Turkish calendar for 1455."

Maria: *Sieben Freuden Mariae, no. 59.*

Matthias de Cracovia, *no. 35.*

Mentelin, Johann. *See nos. 155, 205n.*

Missale abbreviatum. See Supplementary Section E: *Undated Imprints unassigned, no. [6].*

Missale speciale. See Supplementary Section E: *Undated Imprints unassigned, no. [7].*

Nicolas de Lyre. *See* Nicolaus de Lyra.

Nicolaus V, *Pont. Max., nos. 8, 9, 10, 11.*

Nicolaus de Hanapis, *no. 85n.*

Nicolaus de Lyra, *no. 142.*

Nider, Johann, *nos. 80n, 142b. See also* Supplementary Section E: *Undated Imprints re-assigned, no. [68].*

Nijder, Hansen. *See* Nider, Johann.

Pablo de Santa Maria, *no. 205.*

Palladini de Teramo, Jacopo. *See* Jacobus de Theramo.

Parentucelli, Tommaso. *See* Nicolaus V, *Pont. Max.*

Passione di Cristo, no. 57.

Pater noster. See Abecedarium.

Paulus de Sancto Maria. *See* Pablo de Santa Maria.

Petrarca, Francesco. *See* Appendix B, *no. 8.*

Petrus Lombardus, *nos. 143, 212n.*

Phalaris, *no. 144.*

Piccolomini, Eneas Sylvio. *See* Pius II, *Pont. Max.*

Pindarus Thebanus. *See* Appendix B, *no. 9.*

Pius II, *Pont. Max.:*

Breve, nos. 41–44.

Bulla, nos. 42, 46, 47, 64a, 64b.

Epistola ad Mahumetem, no. 207.

Indulgentia, nos. 48, 49, 58, 58b, 94. [*See also no. 206* and Appendix B, *nos. 10, 11.*]

Planet-table [*German*], *no. 24.*

Planetentafel für Laienastrologen. See Planet-table.

Plinius Secundus, Gaius (*Pliny, the Elder*), *no. 208.*

Poggius Florentinus. *See* Appendix B, *no. 8 n.*

III

Pontano, Ludovico (Pontanus), *jurist*. *See* Appendix B, *no. 12*.

Porphyrios (Porphyrius). *See* Appendix B, *no. 13*.

Precatio, no. 17.

Printers and Printing Towns. *See* Supplementary Section: Typographical analysis.

Printers' strike, Basel. *See no. 128n*.

Printing, Invention of. *See* Preface *and* Appendix A.

Proof-sheet and corrections, *no. 140n*.

Psalmi poenitentiales [*Dutch*]. *See* Appendix B, *no. 14*.

Psalter: Cantica, no. 12.

Psalterium Benedictinum, no. 27.

Psalterium Romanum, no. 18.

Puer, Medieval definition of, *no. 87n*.

Rabanus Maurus, *no. 115*.

Radulphus, *nos. 69, 116*.

Respice domine, no. 19.

Rodericus Zamorensis, *no. 145*.

Roman type, *no. 115n*.

Rome, Church of: Cancellaria apostolica, *no. 20*.

Saaz, Johannes von, *nos. 29n, 61n*.

Saliceto, Guilielmus de (Saliceti). *See* Appendix B, *no. 15*.

Sanchez de Arévalo, Rodrigo. *See* Rodericus Zamorensis.

Schoeffer, Peter:

Handbill, *no. 209*.

Status:

As *clericus, nos. 26, 51 and* Appendix A:1(1455).

As *puer, nos. 73n, 87n*.

As engraver. *See* Appendix A:2 (1468).

As printer. *See* Supplementary Section D:2.

As promoter, *no. 209*. *See* Appendix A:2 (1468).

Seneca, Lucius Annaeus. *See* Supplementary Section E: *Undated Imprints re-assigned, no.* [*65*].

Servius Maurus, Honoratus, *no. 210*.

Sibyllenbuch, no. 2.

Sieben Freuden Mariae, no. 59b.

Silius Italicus. *See* Appendix B, *no. 9 n*.

Speculum, Printer of the. *See* Appendix B, *no. 16 n*.

Speculum humanae salvationis. *See* Appendix B, *no. 16*.

Strabo (Strabon), *no. 211*.

Teramo, Jacopo Palladini de. *See* Jacobus de T[h]eramo.

Thomas Aquinas, *St.*:

De articulis fidei et ecclesiae sacramentis, nos. 28, 117.

Summa theologica, Pars prima, no. 146.

Summa theologica, Pars secunda, secunda pars, nos. 66b, 118.

Super quarto libro Sententiarum, no. 212.

Torquemada, Juan de, *no. 119*. *See also* Appendix B, *no. 17*.

Trapezuntinus, Georgius, *no. 92n*.

Trevet, Nicholas. *See* Triveth, Nicolaus.

Triveth, Nicolaus, *no. 147(126)*.

"Turkish calendar for 1455," *no. 5*.

Turrecremata, Joannes de. *See* Torquemada, Juan de.

Type, Compression of, *no. 38n*.

Type specimen-sheet, *no. 209n*.

Urbach, Johannes, *jurist*. *See no. 156n*.

Valla, Lorenzo. *See* Appendix B, *no. 2*.

Valois, Thomas. *See* Waleys, Thomas.

Vergilius Maro, Publicus, *nos. 213, 214*.

Vier Historien von Joseph, Daniel, Judith und Hester, no. 60.

Vincent of Beauvais, *no. 115n*.

Vocabularius ex quo, nos. 120, 215.

Waleys, Thomas, *no. 148(126)*.

Weltgericht, no. 2n.